Life as a Clinical Psychologist

What is it really like?

Life as a Clinical Psychologist

What is it really like?

Paul Jenkins

First published in 2020 by Critical Publishing Ltd

British Library Cataloguing in Publication Data
A CIP record for this book is available from the British Library

ISBN: 978-1-913453-37-4

This book is also available in the following e-book formats:
MOBI ISBN: 978-1-913453-38-1
EPUB ISBN: 978-1-913453-39-8
Adobe e-book ISBN: 978-1-913453-40-4

Cover design by Out of House
Text design by Greensplash Limited
Project Management by Newgen Publishing UK
Printed and bound in Great Britain by 4edge, Essex

Critical Publishing
3 Connaught Road
St Albans
AL3 5RX

www.criticalpublishing.com

Paper from responsible sources

For Peyton, and for Isla

Contents

Student Minds

2% of royalties from sales of *Life as a Clinical Psychologist: What is it Really Like?* by Paul Jenkins will be donated to Student Minds.

Student Minds is the UK's student mental health charity. We empower students and members of the university community to develop the knowledge, confidence and skills to look after their own mental health, support others and create change.

We train students and staff in universities across the UK to deliver student-led peer support interventions as well as research-driven campaigns and workshops. By working collaboratively across sectors, we share best practice and ensure that the student voice influences decisions about student mental health.

Together we will transform the state of student mental health so that all in higher education can thrive.

Meet the author

Paul Jenkins

Paul is currently Associate Professor of Clinical Psychology at the University of Reading and Programme Director for the MSc Theory and Practice in Clinical Psychology, personally delivering teaching on cognitive behaviour therapy and psychopathology. He is an accredited cognitive and behavioural psychotherapist and has also worked in the NHS for over a decade as an applied psychologist. He is an Associate Fellow of the British Psychological Society and has published a number of peer-reviewed journal articles.

Preface

The profession of Clinical Psychology is perpetually fascinating, rewarding, and enjoyable. Although others might argue to the contrary (and, really, who doesn't want to be an astronaut?), for me at least, being a clinical psychologist provides everything I could want in a career. It is challenging, engaging, frustrating at times, and deeply moving. However, my 15 years or so of experience in the field have led me to believe that it is not for everyone. Despite some excellent books charting the path to becoming a clinical psychologist and several textbooks on the subject, too few individuals ask themselves 'what does it mean to be a clinical psychologist, and do I really want to be one?'

This book describes life as a clinical psychologist and aims to help individuals who might aspire to work in the field to consider whether it is right for them, and what alternatives exist if they decide that it might not be. It is not a manual for securing a place on a training course (see, for example, Knight, 2002) but rather aims to provide a balanced view on what it's like to work as a clinical psychologist, putting this into the wider career perspective.

The idea behind this book was to provide an overview of life 'in the trenches' as a clinical psychologist so that people looking to get into, or who are otherwise interested in, the field can learn more about what Clinical Psychology is. Several books exist that describe the empirical side of Clinical Psychology – psychological models of health, appraising the evidence, and so on – but few tell of what the 'day to day' is like.

In the UK, at present, the route to becoming a clinical psychologist takes one necessarily through a doctoral course (previously Master's level until the early 1990s). I enjoyed my doctoral training which, while demanding, was a unique experience and prepared me for working as a clinical psychologist – principally within the NHS. Time since qualifying has been equally demanding and no less interesting. Parts of my career will be referenced through this book in order to provide examples of the type of work that is done, but clinical case examples appear infrequently. Those who wish to read a more complete overview of case studies during clinical training are directed to Tanya Byron's *The Skeleton Cupboard*.

The book itself contains a number of reflective points, brief summaries, and exercises. These are provided as a stimulus to help you think about Clinical Psychology as a career, and to reflect on your own experiences, strengths, and weaknesses. This structure mirrors much of what it is like to practise as a clinical psychologist, but also highlights the difficulty of summarising the profession even in a book. Clinical psychologists, as we will see, have varied careers and work in any number of environments; summarising the 'typical' case is difficult. The intent behind this book is that it can sit alongside Clinical Psychology textbooks, practitioner accounts, and patient views to paint a fuller picture of this diverse profession.

Finally, although an individual perspective is taken throughout this book, it could not have been possible without the support of many individuals – only some of whom are named here. First, Di has cast a professional eye over drafts of this book and I am grateful to the team at Critical Publishing for supporting me in this endeavour. Several colleagues and friends have also provided direct support through revising parts of the book and contributing their own stories to provide a richer account of the profession. Sincere and heartfelt thanks go explicitly to: Cat, Emily, George, Jess, and Renee – outstanding colleagues and friends who have enriched this book through their input, although responsibility for any errors are mine. There were others who had a more 'indirect' role and shaped this book through the impressions made on me throughout my training. I am grateful to the whole staff team on the training course at the University of Southampton (Peter and Alison stick out), Jackie (a fantastic researcher and supervisor), and Caroline (for getting me on the road). Perhaps most influential, however, were all the patients with whom it has quite simply been a privilege to work. Although the role of the clinical psychologist often means that 'face-to-face' work is a small part of my week, you have taught me more than I could ever have learned in textbooks or in meetings, so thank you.

Finally, I need to thank my family for supporting me to do my work and, most recently, for affording me the time to work on this book, when I was also needed as a father, husband, brother, son, and friend.

All that remains is to wish you well in reading this book and to express my hope that it contributes to a long, fascinating, and rewarding career – within Clinical Psychology or elsewhere.

REFERENCES

Byron, T (2015) *The Skeleton Cupboard*. London: Macmillan.

Knight, A (2002) *How to Become a Clinical Psychologist: Getting a Foot in the Door*. Hove, East Sussex: Routledge.

1 Introduction

This book is neither intended to be a memoir (how grandiose!) nor an instruction manual – as we will see, this profession isn't really like that. In spite of this (and the recurring use of the first person), I have tried to avoid excessive pretention and self-focus, and also to limit the amount of 'you must do X in order to get to Y…'. However, the primary goal of this book is to introduce what Clinical Psychology really is, and what life is like as a practising clinical psychologist, although it will also cover the stages of training in some detail.

You may have picked this book up as a student in the early stages of your career, as someone in contact with clinical psychologists (as a patient, collaborator, or colleague), or simply as someone who is interested in knowing more about a career that has seen consistently high numbers of applications to postgraduate training over recent years. The book will describe my own experiences, supplemented by those of other professionals and through reference to published articles and other sources of information. Case illustrations are used at times to emphasise points, the details of which have been changed to protect the identity of the individuals involved.

WHAT IS A CLINICAL PSYCHOLOGIST?

There is some confusion about what exactly a clinical psychologist is, and what they do. Clinical psychologists are healthcare professionals who are trained in psychological theories and treatments and apply these to health problems. However, explaining the exact role of a clinical psychologist isn't easy – we work in many different settings, practise in different ways, and treat a wide range of people with an even wider range of presenting problems. As other writers in this area have noted (eg, Llewelyn and Aafjes-van Doorn, 2017), we are not mind-readers and we are not constantly analysing people. (Well, at least no more than most.) To add depth to these experiences, the perspectives of two colleagues are presented later in the book to offer different views on working as a clinical psychologist. The first, by Jess (Chapter 3), discusses the experience of what the first job after training is like. Georgina (Chapter 5) then talks about working in a specialist Clinical Health Psychology setting, and reflects on issues ranging from team working to self-care.

Training in Clinical Psychology is based on a grounding in general psychology (usually reflected by an undergraduate degree in Psychology) and then advanced (postgraduate) education through a mix of practical experience and further academic study. The key tenets of training will be discussed throughout the book and particularly the idea that

Clinical Psychology is based on a 'reflective scientist practitioner' model, meaning that practitioners blend a scientific (or empirical) approach with one that pays greater attention to self-awareness and reviewing one's own practice.

Once trained, there are many paths a clinical psychologist's career can take. With the majority of clinical psychologists working in healthcare, a key employer in the UK is the National Health Service (NHS). A qualified clinical psychologist working for the NHS will generally be responsible for a caseload of individuals as well as engaging with a range of work such as providing support to others, training staff, and service evaluation. Some illustrative examples – linked to level of seniority within the profession – are provided in Figure 1.1, but these will vary according to the setting and, of course, are likely to vary over time.

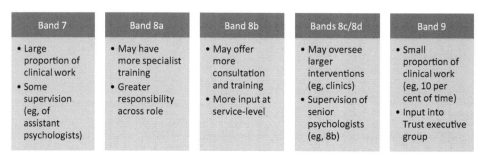

Figure 1.1 Examples of differences in range of work between different grades (Agenda for Change bands) of clinical psychologist.
Note: this is illustrative and more details can be found in BPS (2012).

USING THE TITLE *CLINICAL PSYCHOLOGIST*

In common with other roles within both applied psychology (eg, health psychologist, counselling psychologist) and other healthcare professions (eg, dietitian, occupational therapist), the term *clinical psychologist* is a protected title. That means that the title is protected by law such that those using the term must be appropriately registered; in the UK, all clinical psychologists are currently regulated by the Health and Care Professions Council (HCPC). The purpose of this regulation is, in large part, to protect the public and requires its registrants to meet certain criteria to continue to practise. In addition to standards of proficiency, organisations such as the HCPC also publish standards of conduct and ethics by which practitioners must abide (this is discussed more in Chapter 4). In order to identify individuals at a pre-qualification stage, those in training may use a prefix such as 'trainee' or 'student'.

However, such legislation is not present in some areas of the world, and the training requirements – in Clinical Psychology, for example – are not identical to those in the UK. Many nations are in the process of developing Clinical Psychology services, which is often responsive to population need as well as educational conventions and the way healthcare is funded. As such, training varies widely across the world with countries and regions where Clinical Psychology is more established (eg, Europe and the USA) representing only a fraction of the world's population. Clinical Psychology appears to be a growing profession globally, but its delivery also reflects the society in which it is developing.

Rather confusingly, some related titles are not protected in the UK, including the generic title 'psychologist'. There are reasons for this, the principal one being that a protected title includes defining a number of related competencies (see Chapter 3) and that doing this for a field as wide as general psychology would be impractical but also perhaps so wide-ranging as to be meaningless (Murphy, 2008). Unclear use of titles can cause confusion for students of psychology, as well as the public at large so it is important to understand a little about why this is so.

We shall explore the role, training, and development of clinical psychologists throughout this book and will also look at what makes clinical psychologists unique. To start with, however, I will try to summarise what a typical day might look like for a clinical psychologist.

A DAY IN THE LIFE

In many respects, the day of a clinical psychologist is not unlike that of many other professionals. We go to work and this is usually within 'sociable hours', Monday to Friday.[1] We dress smartly but not stuffily. We tend to work mostly in offices, although the scenery will often change from a therapy room to a shared office to a board room to a patient's home. And here, I feel, is where we begin to see some of the essence of Clinical Psychology.

I am lucky enough to have an office. However, throughout my career I have conducted my business in dilapidated meeting rooms large enough to fit 30 adults, a lounge with two frisky canines marauding in the room next door, virtual reality suites with technology that can quite literally make one's head spin, the busy corridors of a general hospital, and beneath an oak tree on a warm day, to name just a few. I have also chosen, and been lucky enough, to specialise in eating disorders – a field that has struck fear, or at least apprehension, into the hearts of many a resilient practitioner. The focus of this book is on Clinical Psychology as a *gestalt*, but the stories within are necessarily tinged by the thread of this particular clinical specialism that has run through my career. However, to take this field as an example, clinical psychologists might share meals with patients in a hospital dining room, eat snacks at Starbucks (other coffee retailers are available), participate in a therapeutic meal at a restaurant, and run groups on how to make sensible and healthy meal choices. They are also likely to offer consultation to staff less experienced in the field and provide training to those looking to learn more. All may seem ordinary, even mundane, at first glance but, in the context of the psychologist's role with the patients and staff involved, the level of complexity runs much deeper.

---

1 I feel I ought to note here that many of my statements refer to the 'norm' and I freely admit that there are many exceptions to the rule. To those people, I apologise, as it is not my intent to ignore the differences across practice in this wide discipline.

As these allegories hopefully illustrate, Clinical Psychology is not for the faint-hearted. In my experience, those who fare best with the rigours of practice are flexible, open-minded, reflective, resilient, and astute. A sense of humour is far from ubiquitous, but it certainly helps. Chapter 2 aims to explore the qualities that might make for a successful clinical psychologist in more detail, but before that we shall look at an overall summary of Clinical Psychology and a bit about my own journey.

Dinner conversations with friends (an indicator of my age perhaps) will often cover issues around our respective careers. My enthusiasm for my work is contrasted with friends in other jobs who admit that, were they not paid the amount they are, they might consider a change in track. I have friends who regularly exceed a 40-hour week and are called in at late notice to meet a deadline, and this is understood as being 'part of the job'. There are certainly many clinical psychologists who work in excess of their salaried hours (see Longwill, 2015), and any clinical psychologists reading this book might think 'who doesn't?' However, we are seldom asked to work 'through the night' or to sacrifice time set aside for our personal lives to trudge – sorry, come – into the office. However, by no means should that be taken to imply that clinical psychologists do not, from time to time, exceed what might be reasonably expected of them. We sometimes fulfil the role of a 'duty worker' and can be involved in providing out-of-hours cover, but usually far less than colleagues from Nursing or Medicine will report. The point of this is that Clinical Psychology does not suffer much of the stress of 'city careers' or the near-omnipresent risks of a life in the Armed Forces, but it does demand commitment and a willingness to 'go the extra mile'.

As we will see later, one of the strengths of applied psychology is its widespread endorsement of reflective practice. This is seen by many as one of the competencies of clinical psychologists – the ability to reflect on one's own practice 'in the moment' and using this self-awareness to inform decision-making (Beinart et al, 2009). Such an approach is often incompatible with expedited ('emergency') reviews, although clinical psychologists will often provide useful input in such instances. Reflective practice (which is commonly associated with greater self-awareness, holding of therapeutic boundaries, and continuous development) provides a great deal of unspoken containment and assurance, features that many will recognise as necessary for safe and effective practice.

This emphasis on insight and self-reflection can have costs, however. On occasion, I have worked 'too hard' on a given day and found myself exhausted at the end of it. The weariness of a 'rough day at the office' can be felt deep within – it is an emotional exhaustion that can come from bearing too many troubles or spinning too many plates. This may sound like too much psychology mumbo-jumbo and that the 'woe is me' has started already, but one of the main purposes of this book would be lost if it boasted only of the highs and covered none of the lows. Perhaps important to note here is that, if you feel that you are someone who struggles with emotional stress or is adversely affected by hearing the lamentations of others, this might prompt some questions in your mind about your desired profession.

THE SETTINGS IN WHICH CLINICAL PSYCHOLOGISTS WORK

Clinical psychologists can be found in a wide range of environments – from those one might expect (such as mental health teams based in the community) to those that seem less intuitive (such as designing video games or encouraging innovation with NASA; see www.apa.org/action/index.aspx). The most popular in the UK are summarised below.

1.1: RESEARCH SUMMARY

Where do clinical psychologists work?

Around 80 per cent of UK clinical psychologists undertake at least some work in the specialisms listed below. These data are taken from Longwill (2015) and, as many clinical psychologists work across more than one area, the total number exceeds 100 per cent.

- o Adult Mental Health (around 41 per cent)
- o Child and Family (around 30 per cent)
- o Learning Disabilities (around 21 per cent)
- o Clinical Health Psychology (around 18 per cent)
- o Neuropsychology (around 20 per cent)
- o Older Adults (around 12 per cent)
- o Forensic (around 10 per cent)
- o Paediatric Psychology (around 11 per cent)
- o Management (around 12 per cent)

Despite the wide diffusion of clinical psychologists across organisational settings, the NHS remains the largest employer of clinical psychologists in the UK. Combined with my own experience, the effect on this book is that issues around healthcare are typically foremost in the discussion. I have tried to use illustrations and examples from other fields where possible but concede that I have not been able to cover all possible eventualities when considering careers in Clinical Psychology.

CLINICAL WORK... AND MORE

Although providing psychological therapy is often, and appropriately, seen as an important role of the clinical psychologist, this is only one aspect to the job and those looking to become clinical psychologists would benefit from being aware of this (as this has not always been my experience when talking to aspiring clinical psychologists). The modern clinical psychologist will often work not only with patients but staff as well (see Research Summary 1.2).

1.2: RESEARCH SUMMARY

What can clinical psychologists offer to hospice care?

A study by Russell and Fountain (2018) sought the views of clinical and counselling psychologists working in UK hospice settings (ie, services which generally support people with end-of-life, or palliative, care). Alongside direct work with patients, psychologists reported frequently engaging in 'group supervision/ reflective practice', 'debriefing following critical incidents', and 'facilitating psychoeducational groups'. A range of therapeutic approaches were reported, such as cognitive behaviour therapy, narrative therapy, and systemic therapy, and many also used feedback to improve their practice.

Source: Russell and Fountain (2018)

Given their skills in formulation and reflective practice, clinical psychologists might offer group supervision to staff in a busy clinical environment in order to help people 'step back' and consider the best course of action in a given situation. Considering the complexities of such work, this often means discussing a range of different ideas rather than the clinical psychologist determining the 'right' course of action.

We will cover different features of the clinical psychologist's role throughout the book, but common aspects, in addition to clinical work, include input into service evaluation and quality improvement, teaching, consultation and leadership, and research (see Chapter 8). Psychologists often consult with other professionals (such as medical doctors, other allied healthcare professionals, and teachers) and therefore may provide opinion, information, or advice based on limited contact with the 'patient'. For example, a comprehensive assessment of a child's needs may include a clinical psychologist talking with teaching staff and educational psychologists about school performance, paediatricians about any underlying medical issues, or social workers about wider circumstances, all before speaking with the child or their parents.

Similarly, supervision of other staff is often provided by clinical psychologists. Recipients of supervision can include 'junior' psychologists (which may include managerial responsibility as well) as well as those from other professions who can benefit from the knowledge and experience of a clinical psychologist. Given the clinical psychologist's education in psychotherapy models, supervising staff delivering psychological interventions is a common aspect to the work and can be provided in both group and individual settings. More specific supervision – such as that of a particular therapeutic model or research supervision – might sit alongside generic clinical supervision.

There is also a lot of indirect clinical work that happens in health services. For example, I used to screen all the referrals for our clinic in order to determine their risk and whether they were appropriate for our service. Often, this involved calling GPs (who were our most frequent referrers) to get more information or liaising with staff in other teams to see which would be the most appropriate service for the patient's needs. Patients who had been assessed would then be discussed in a team meeting (another of my roles was to chair this) in order to determine the most appropriate treatment plan. Some cases were relatively straightforward and could be allocated to a treatment based on national guidance, whereas others necessitated a more complex management plan, often involving professionals from different groups and services.

One role that is undertaken by a number of professional groups working in mental health is known within the UK as 'care co-ordination'. Implemented as part of the Care Programme Approach (or CPA), this involves monitoring of a patient's care and co-ordinating support, often across services. The care co-ordinator will agree a 'care plan' with the patient (and family or carers, where indicated) and regularly review the care that is offered.

As seen in Figure 1.2, a patient can have contact with a great number of different professionals, and lack of co-ordination is likely to lead to patients' needs not being met, greater

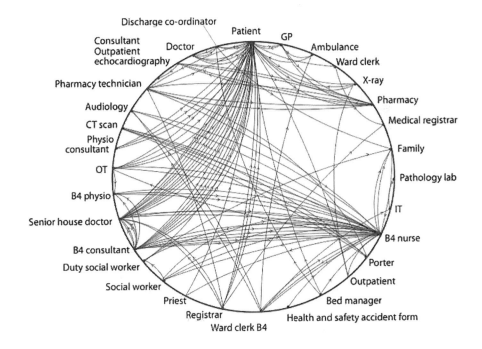

Figure 1.2 Multidisciplinary working in complex cases: diagram indicating the number of staff elements involved in one discharge of a particularly complex patient.
(Jones and Mitchell, 2006, p 12. Reprinted with permission from the NHS Confederation, Lean Thinking for the NHS. NHS Confederation, 2006)

expense, and poor quality of care (see Øvretveit, 2011). The British Psychological Society recommends that clinical psychologists act as care co-ordinators, but principally where there is a '*strong psychological aspect*' to the case (BPS, 2012, p 16). However, even when not acting as a care co-ordinator or working directly with patients, clinical psychologists often play a pivotal role, contributing in many different ways to an individual's care.

DEMOGRAPHICS OF UK CLINICAL PSYCHOLOGISTS

To establish an accurate profile of clinical psychologists working in the UK, a report was commissioned by the Division of Clinical Psychology (DCP) of the British Psychological Society (BPS) and published in November 2015 (Longwill, 2015). The results indicated that around 80 per cent of clinical psychologists are female, with a mean age of 42 years. An estimated 15 per cent of clinical psychologists are employed outside of their main role (including self-employment), and the numbers registering as clinical psychologists generally exceeds the numbers deregistering, suggesting continued growth (Farndon, nd).

The distribution of clinical psychologists across the UK, however, is not uniform. As illustrated in Figure 1.3, England hosts the majority of registered clinical psychologists and sits, with Scotland, above the average per 100,000 population. Wales and Northern Ireland have lower numbers of clinical psychologists in proportion to their respective populations (Longwill, 2015). Within this, certain areas of the UK report different coverage, with Greater London typically having proportionally more clinical psychologists and East Anglia having the fewest (Farndon, nd).

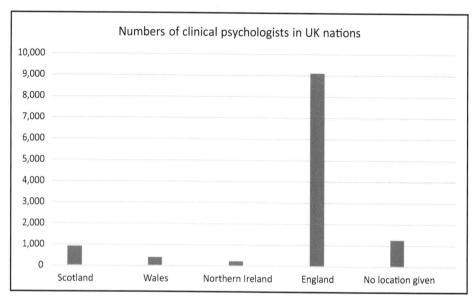

Figure 1.3 The Clinical Psychology workforce in the UK.
(Adapted from Longwill, 2015)

As various studies of clinical psychologists suggest, the profession is overwhelmingly female and, typically, underrepresented across minority groups. However, many of the 'pioneers' in the field are men (usually White men), and, although many influential female figures have played important roles in its development, they occupy fewer pages in the history books (Pilgrim et al, 2015). There is some evidence that this is beginning to change, however, and we will return to the subject of diversity in Clinical Psychology later in this book.

A BRIEF HISTORY OF CLINICAL PSYCHOLOGY

The popularity of Clinical Psychology has been relatively enduring during my professional lifetime. A discipline that can trace its modern origins to the last few years of the nineteenth century, Clinical Psychology has always been closely allied with Medicine, both sharing the goal of helping others, and doing so upon a strong empirical, or scientific, foundation (Routh, 2010). Indeed, early mentions of 'clinical psychology' overlap with medical teaching – known now as the discipline of psychiatry (eg, Crichton-Browne, 1861) – and many concepts discussed in the early nineteenth century, including compassion and appropriate training in psychology, will be familiar today (eg, see Browne, 1837).

Clinical Psychology developed from more general 'scientific' psychology, blending this approach with the clinical traditions of psychotherapy and the evolution of psychometric testing (Hall et al, 2015). It is difficult to trace its exact origins, but evolution of Clinical Psychology in the UK mirrored that in the USA to some extent (although there was some cross-fertilisation), and advancement in both was seemingly accelerated by the two World Wars, as society had to deal with the mental scars that global armed conflict left behind. The complex web of cultural, political, and socioeconomic changes at this time saw some '*psychological activity in clinical settings*' (Pilgrim et al, 2015, p 370) and the profession continued to progress in the post-war years.

Postgraduate clinical training was first established in the late 1940s and early 1950s (see Hall et al, 2015), its evolution closely linked with the development of the NHS, which was itself launched in July 1948. Clinical Psychology then began to establish more of a foothold in healthcare through its association with the empirical method and role in the care of children in particular (Stewart, 2015). Its growth continued into the 1980s and 1990s, alongside recognition of the shortage of clinical psychologists.

The training curriculum for clinical psychologists also began to shift at this time to a model that resembles the current training structure and, by the mid-1990s, most courses offered Clinical Psychology doctorates (Turpin, 1995). Alongside the push towards evidence-based practice seen at this time, the last few decades have also been associated with managerialism within the NHS, providing an opportunity for greater self-government within Clinical Psychology, but also changes to the routine 'job description' of the clinical psychologist. This approach created an '*accountability hierarchy*' within the profession and, although this doesn't always reflect the managerial line of sight, this had a significant impact on clinical psychologists working in the NHS (Pilgrim and Patel, 2015).

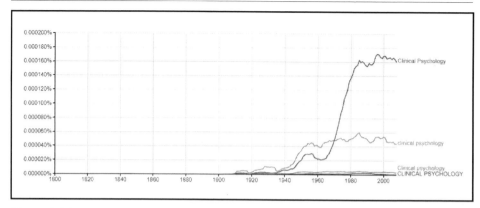

Figure 1.4 Graph of frequency of usage of 'Clinical Psychology' in books from 1800 to 2017. *(© Michel et al, 2011 via Google Books Ngram Viewer; http://books.google.com/ngrams)*

Interested readers are advised to consult the extensively researched and detailed *Clinical Psychology in Britain: Historical Perspectives* by Hall and colleagues (2015). Understanding the history of Clinical Psychology gives insight into many of the struggles the profession faces today. For example, for some time it has not been clear whether clinical psychologists are scientists or practitioners, a debate to which we shall return later in this book. The recent shift in emphasis on leadership roles and advanced clinical competence will likely mean a corresponding shift in the structure of training, with doctoral programmes looking to evolve in line with the needs of modern healthcare. It is remarkable that Hall et al, given their extensive review of Clinical Psychology (alongside their wealth of experience), also reflect that the clinical psychologist's *'true identity'* has often seemed elusive. Future generations will ultimately shape the course of this profession but it would be wise to heed the lessons of the past.

TRAINING OUTSIDE OF THE UK

Clinical psychologists in other countries will have different experiences to those trained in the UK. In Europe, for example, there is a more diverse range of employers and the private sector is a larger stakeholder (relative to the UK) within many European nations. Some countries have a greater reliance on supervised practice, with trainee psychologists completing a postgraduate course and then engaging in closely supervised practice. For example, in Iceland, after completing a Master's degree (or equivalent), individuals must work for 12 months under the supervision of a senior psychologist before applying for permission to practise. However, the general structure of training (ie, a related undergraduate degree followed by practical training with academic demands) is fairly universal. The NHS (UK) training of a clinical psychologist tends to be generic, with education across a number of core areas (see Chapter 3). Reflecting the more diversified employment arrangements (McPherson, 1992), Clinical Psychology training in Europe often has a greater focus on specialised training, such as in certain branches of psychotherapy.

In Ireland, a country with close links to the UK, training also follows a three-year doctoral course and some studies have reported demographics of practising clinical psychologists (eg, Carr, 1995). The history of Clinical Psychology in Ireland has also been well-documented and is particularly fascinating given its strong links to Catholicism in the early days of its founding (see Carr, 2015). Currently, Clinical Psychology programmes are delivered in partnership between a university and the Health Services Executive (HSE), which is responsible for delivery of clinical placements, and accredited by the Psychological Society of Ireland. Applicants must show a strong academic record (eg, a good undergraduate degree and, often, an additional degree in a related area), have experience in a clinical area, as well as the personal aptitude to practise as a clinical psychologist. The career structure of clinical psychologists in Ireland mirrors that of the UK, with trainee, basic, senior, principal and director grades, and its development continues alongside a political focus on mental health (Carr, 2015).

The training of clinical psychologists in the US (and Canada) is (rather confusingly when compared to UK terminology) via a PhD route. PhD programmes in Clinical Psychology provide both clinical and research training (similar to the DClinPsychol equivalent in the UK) and lead to licensure within a particular state or province. Training in North America, as in the UK, is extremely popular. For example, in 2013, over 50 per cent of psychology Master's degrees and doctorates in the USA were in clinical, counselling, or educational psychology (Clay, 2017).

The PsyD degree emerged in the 1970s as an acceptable alternative to the PhD, which has less of an emphasis on research skills although comprises similar components (including a doctoral-level project). Both routes require a given number of hours to be conducted in practice, which is predominantly clinical (some 'research hours' can be counted). Following a suitable degree (eg, PhD), candidates for licensure in the US typically engage in one year's 'internship' training and further 'postdoctoral' training (sometimes up to four years). This does vary across states, however, and culminates in the Examination for Professional Practice in Psychology (EPPP), passing of which makes the candidate eligible for licensure. In Canada, there is a similar process (usually including the EPPP), although some provinces mandate a minimum of doctoral training for licensure as a 'psychologist' whereas, in others, individuals with Master's degrees in Clinical Psychology can be registered.

Although there are differences in the models used to train clinical psychologists across countries, a number of similarities recur, such as the importance of training in both research and practice, an understanding of broader human psychology, and an appreciation of professional ethics. Within the UK, at least, training for clinical psychologists is broadly similar – for this, and other reasons mentioned above, this book will consider the practice of Clinical Psychology in the UK as its primary focus although many of the themes and ideas will be applicable to other parts of the world.

LOOKING FORWARDS

This introduction has summarised the interest and breadth of Clinical Psychology as a career choice. We have touched on some areas (for example, how to become a clinical psychologist, where clinical psychologists work, and what alternatives there might be) that will be covered in more detail in later chapters. I hope you feel sufficiently interested to read on, and that what follows can answer many of the questions that you might have. The next chapter considers Clinical Psychology in more detail, and will cover important aspects of the role, such as providing psychological therapy, evidence-based practice, and formulation.

REFERENCES

Beinart, H, Llewelyn, S and Kennedy, P (2009) Competency Approaches, Ethics and Partnerships in Clinical Psychology. In Beinart, H, Llewelyn, S and Kennedy, P (eds), *Clinical Psychology in Practice* (pp 18–32). Chichester: Wiley-Blackwell.

British Psychological Society (BPS) (2012) Guidelines on Activity for Clinical Psychologists. [online] Available at: www.bps.org.uk/sites/www.bps.org.uk/files/Member%20Networks/Divisions/DCP/Guidelines%20of%20 Activity%20for%20CP%27s.pdf (accessed 6 July 2020).

Browne, W A F (1837) What Asylums Were, Are, and Ought to Be: Being the Substance of Five Lectures Delivered before the Managers of the Montrose Royal Lunatic Asylum. Edinburgh: Adam and Charles Black. [online] Available at: https://archive.org/details/whatasylumswerea02brow/page/n2/mode/2up (accessed 6 July 2020).

Carr, A (1995) Clinical Psychology in Ireland: A National Survey. *The Irish Journal of Psychology*, 16(1): 1–20.

Carr, A (2015) The Development of Clinical Psychology in the Republic of Ireland. In Hall, J, Pilgrim, D and Turpin, G (eds), *Clinical Psychology in Britain: Historical Perspectives* (pp 342–8). Leicester: BPS.

Clay, R A (2017) Trends Report: Psychology is More Popular than Ever. *Monitor on Psychology*, 48: 10. [online] Available at: www.apa.org/monitor/2017/11/trends-popular (accessed 6 July 2020).

Crichton-Browne, J (1861) *The Clinical Teaching of Psychology: A Valedictory Address*. Edinburgh: James Nichol. [online] Available at: https://wellcomecollection.org/works/xt4tfvkh (accessed 6 July 2020).

Farndon, H (nd) HCPC Registered Psychologists in the UK. [online] Available at: www.bps.org.uk/sites/www. bps.org.uk/files/Policy/Policy%20-%20Files/HCPC%20Registered%20Psychologists%20in%20the%20UK. pdf (accessed 6 July 2020).

Good, B, Walsh, R M, Alexander, G and Moore, G (2014) Assessment of the Acute Psychiatric Patient in the Emergency Department: Legal Cases and Caveats. *Western Journal of Emergency Medicine*, 15: 312–17.

Hall, J, Pilgrim, D and Turpin, G (2015) *Clinical Psychology in Britain: Historical Perspectives*. Leicester: BPS.

Jones, D and Mitchell, A (2006) Lean Thinking for the NHS. [online] Available at: www.nhsconfed.org/-/media/ Confederation/Files/Publications/Documents/Lean-thinking-for-the-NHS.pdf (accessed 6 July 2020).

Llewelyn, S and Aafjes-van Doorn, K (2017) *Clinical Psychology: A Very Short Introduction*. Oxford: Oxford University Press.

Longwill, A (2015) Clinical Psychology Workforce Project Division of Clinical Psychology UK. [online] Available at: www.bps.org.uk/sites/www.bps.org.uk/files/Page%20-%20Files/Clinical%20Psychology%20 Workforce%20Report%20%282015%29.pdf (accessed 6 July 2020).

McPherson, F M (1992) Clinical Psychology Training in Europe. *British Journal of Clinical Psychology*, 31: 419–28.

Michel, J B, et al (2011) Quantitative Analysis of Culture Using Millions of Digitized Books. *Science*, 331(6014): 176–82.

Murphy, D (2008) As Good as It Gets. *The Psychologist*, 21: 344–7.

Øvretveit, J (2011) *Does Clinical Coordination Improve Quality and Save Money?* London, UK: Health Foundation. [online] Available at: www.health.org.uk/sites/default/files/DoesClinicalCoordinationImproveQualityAndSaveMoneyVol2_fullversion.pdf (accessed 6 July 2020).

Pilgrim, D and Patel, N (2015) The Emergence of Clinical Psychology in the British Post-War Context. In Hall, J, Pilgrim, D and Turpin, G (eds), *Clinical Psychology in Britain: Historical Perspectives* (pp 52–64). Leicester: BPS.

Pilgrim, D, Turpin, G and Hall, J (2015) Overview: Recurring Themes and Continuing Challenges. In Hall, J, Pilgrim, D and Turpin, G (eds), *Clinical Psychology in Britain: Historical Perspectives* (pp 365–78). Leicester: BPS.

Routh, D K (2010) A History of Clinical Psychology. In Barlow, D H (ed), *The Oxford Handbook of Clinical Psychology*. Oxford: Oxford University Press.

Russell, C and Fountain, A (2018) Role of Clinical Psychology in UK Hospices. *BMJ Supportive & Palliative Care*. DOI: 10.1136/bmjspcare-2018-001594.

Stewart, J (2015) Psychology in Context: From the First World War to the National Health Service. In Hall, J, Pilgrim, D and Turpin, G (eds), *Clinical Psychology in Britain: Historical Perspectives* (pp 39–51). Leicester: BPS.

Turpin, G (1995) Practitioner Doctorates in Clinical Psychology. *The Psychologist*, 8(8): 356–8.

2 Do you really want to be a clinical psychologist? *Really*?

I feel that I ought to preface this chapter by saying that it is most assuredly not my intention to sway people *away* from Clinical Psychology. However, I do wish to communicate some of the challenges inherent to the work and aim to provide a relatively unbiased view of life as a clinical psychologist.

A TWO-SIDED COIN

The proportion of trainee clinical psychologists who go on to graduate from professional training courses in Clinical Psychology is very high, so one could reasonably argue that prospective clinical psychologists are sufficiently prepared and informed about the rigours of training. On the other hand, clinical psychologists are also determined folk and the many I have met rarely leave a job half-completed. Thus, the idea of leaving The Course does not come lightly to most. The rigours of training, however, are not without reason: I have either heard about or sadly seen cases where otherwise hardy individuals have been reduced to tears by the emotional demands of their practice. As in many healthcare professions, the reality of life 'at the coalface' can sometimes be as dark and toxic as the metaphor suggests.

Hearing a patient disclose a history of abuse or struggling against pressures and problems that seem insurmountable can generate deep sorrow in even the most robust of individuals. That many along the path of their career confide in friends and loved ones about their troubles is also not unique to this profession. Training to be a clinical psychologist is a bit like a road of yellow brick, complete with perceived impasses, demons, the odd winged monkey (or at least the occasional pet), and, perhaps most importantly, people who just need your help. True to the cognitive-behavioural tradition within which I was trained, we shall do our best to review the evidence and then I invite you to make your own opinion about the merits of this field over others, and the virtue of its approach. I certainly believe that it is right for me, but to assume that to be true in all cases is a stark illustration of what Beck called '*overgeneralisation*'.

So, what is good and bad about being a clinical psychologist? First, some of the negatives. Why not start with money? It's seldom the reason that people get into Clinical Psychology and if it is yours, you may want to rethink. Relative to those working in the other 'helping professions', however, clinical psychologists are generally in a privileged position. Unlike nurses, occupational therapists, and some others, we are, at present, paid by the National Health Service to complete the professional doctorate in Clinical

Psychology although undergraduate Psychology is typically not funded. The pay is pretty healthy and for a Year 1 trainee lies above the 60th percentile for the UK (HMRC, 2020).

What this overlooks is that many people have taken voluntary or 'honorary' positions along their journey and have also taken jobs in lower-paid roles, such as healthcare assistants and support workers, to enable them to get this far. Other people have given up more financially rewarding careers to pursue Clinical Psychology and have thus made a number of tangible sacrifices. Given the necessity of an accredited undergraduate degree and at least some experience, the mean age of first-year trainee clinical psychologists is around 27, although this varies quite substantially (eg, Scior et al, 2014). The issue of honorary psychologist positions is covered more in Chapter 3, but suffice it to say here that many people start out looking for something in the field that is unpaid.

Many clinical psychologists move into different roles during their career. For example, some will undertake specialist training in a certain treatment model and others will pursue management positions. In the current NHS pay system, known as Agenda for Change, or AfC, staff (excluding doctors, dentists, and many senior managers) are allocated to pay bands based on the requirements of their role. Thus, the 'grades' we saw in the last chapter (Figure 1.1) should reflect the knowledge, responsibility, and skills required for their job (NHS Employers, 2019). This arrangement will often mean that clinical psychologists may move jobs in order to advance their careers. Figure 2.1 provides a snapshot of the distribution of clinical psychologists in AfC bands based on data from Longwill (2015).

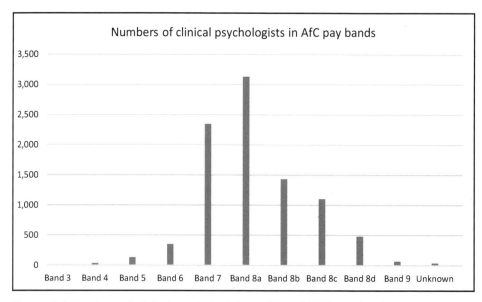

Figure 2.1 Numbers of clinical psychologists in different NHS pay bands.
Note: there are some errors in this data (also acknowledged by Longwill, 2015) as qualified clinical psychologists would rarely, if ever, be employed below Band 7.
(Longwill, 2015, p 63)

As in any career, one starts at, or pretty near, the bottom. Many Psychology graduates find that, once the pride and pomp of their commencement has passed, they struggle to find an identity – or even distinctiveness – among the legions of other aspirant junior psychologists. I have always felt pride in being a psychologist (clinical or otherwise) but this can easily be forgotten after the tenth job application is but a distant memory of a long, interview-free winter. It is also too easy to allow your career to list under the pressures of rejections and to choose a job that might, in some tangential way, get you to where you want to go.

The next chapter covers the routes to Clinical Psychology in more detail, but I shall share a brief anecdote here. I once applied for a job as an assistant psychologist in an area of Clinical Psychology in which I had little-to-no interest (sacrilege, I know), in an area of the country where I had no friends, and was interviewed in a place that seemed bleak and uncompromising. The interview panel were friendly but I left feeling that I didn't really put myself across all that well. Perhaps unsurprisingly, they called me later to let me know that I was unsuccessful. Although initially disappointed, I later came to reflect that being offered this job would have positioned me facing a very difficult choice; would I take a job in a part of the country I didn't know and with no established social contact to get me closer to my goal of doctoral training? It all boiled down to the question of 'how much am I willing to give up?' The good news (at least for me) is that I didn't need to answer those questions. After some time had passed, I was offered a job working with children, had a wonderful supervisor, and was supported to progress to the next stage of my career.

HIGHS AND LOWS

Clinical Psychology can be tough in myriad ways. I have already alluded to the emotional demands of the career, demands that are similar throughout healthcare. (Despite the many applications of Clinical Psychology, the most frequently travelled route is through healthcare.) A friend of mine once told me a story of how a patient's description of a traumatic experience left her so distraught that, after the session, she crawled under her desk and cried for 30 minutes. Patients do not always get better, and there are some people whom you alone simply cannot help; this can seem, at times, soul-destroying.

Clinical Psychology is also academically tough and, as we will cover more in later chapters, the research expertise of clinical psychologists can be used to influence service provision at many levels. The professional degree has a strong emphasis on clinical skills, but also requires completion of a doctoral-level thesis, which usually involves a major research project. A minority of these projects eventually make it into print as scientific articles, albeit with some tailoring, and so the academic bar is set high. The thesis and the associated viva voce (an interview about one's research) have left many a trainee with sleepless nights – for one reason or another.

The three years I spent studying for my doctorate were truly some of the best of my life. However, there were times when deadlines took priority over fun and when '*nah, I have to do some work*' is a genuine reason for not going out. Many trainees feel that their life is on hold, not just for the length of their studies, but also for the many years of training either side of this. Friends of mine have put off house moves and considered family planning based on their stage in Psychology's version of the Tour de France. It can seem as though getting on to, or completing, The Course is singularly the most important thing in one's life. The support of friends and family is vital, but relationships can at times be tested by the rigours of clinical training. This account may not be too different from others who have a strong career focus, but it is a reality of this vocation.

Once qualified – and possibly before – others will look to you for guidance, support, and leadership, typically in difficult situations (after all, when would you otherwise look for such things?). The demands of this can be challenging and your training will go some way to preparing you; however, you will also need to rely on your personal attributes and coping skills. One characteristic that I have often seen in those who cope well with the demands of Clinical Psychology is the ability to think on one's feet. The fact is that patients (or clients, or stakeholders, or colleagues) can be trying, and you may also end up in an unfortunate set of circumstances that compound your predicament. You must be prepared to think on your feet and, if you're not very good at this, you might struggle with some aspects of the role. You should also be supported (by supervisors and colleagues, for example), but this won't always be the case and many decisions will be firmly guided by you.

Although there may be many more negatives to this career than I have touched on, there is a risk that once you reach your goal of becoming a clinical psychologist, you will find it is not all you thought it would be. You are still faced with the difficulties of working in a large health service (if that is the route you choose) and you might not have all the resources you need at your disposal. The work can also be tedious at times and people don't always listen to you and follow your suggestions. Once you have obtained a doctorate, what do you choose to do then? Clinical Psychology is a wonderful career for its variety and the opportunities it affords, and you may wish to change direction in later life. Do you want to work in private practice? Do you want to spend more time starting and growing a family? Do you want to manage a service or be involved in training others? As shown back in Figure 1.1 on page 2, the nature of the workload shifts over time and may not be what you had anticipated. Becoming a clinical psychologist is not the end of the road; it is an essential step in what can produce a fascinating and rewarding career.

So, if that list hasn't put you off, here's some of the good news. As a clinical psychologist, you can really make a difference. It sounds trite but working therapeutically with people in distress affords some of the most satisfying experiences you can have in life, and it is an honour that they come to you for help. To watch someone overcome a mental health problem or develop new ways of seeing the world based on the work that the two of you have done together is immeasurably gratifying. That people come to you and share their deepest fears and hopes is truly a privilege, and to help them reach their own aspirations is endlessly rewarding. Using your knowledge of Psychology and applying it to teams can show the true potential of groups, and your role as a leader in this can be as exciting as it is worthwhile.

For those with a more adventurous nature, clinical psychologists get to work in some of the most varied environments on the planet – alongside armies, governments, hospitals, humanitarian organisations, multinational companies, universities, airlines, schools, and many more. As we will see in the next chapter, achieving the status of a clinical psychologist can lead to employment across the globe. Practice Summary 2.1 describes the management of mental health in people who have presented to general hospital, known as psychological medicine or liaison psychiatry.

2.1: PRACTICE SUMMARY

Psychologists in emergency departments and 'liaison teams'

Psychologists are important members of the liaison team in terms of offering psychological assessments, having input to risk assessments, providing treatment plans and reports, and working with colleagues to consider onwards referral. The route of a patient seeking support for psychiatric problems through the Emergency Department is often complex, including medical clearance, exclusion of organic disease or other underlying causes (eg, medication toxicity), and assessment of psychiatric risk. A patient may present with attempted overdose following an argument and be observed as showing varying levels of mental capacity (see Good et al, 2014).

Frontline staff therefore encounter individuals with risky presentations for whom no physical cause is present that can be immediately treated, and who may require transfer to mental health services and support from a mental health professional (including clinical psychologists). In such circumstances, a psychologist might review an individual who is admitted to the hospital (perhaps against the patient's will) and aim to assist the patient in trying to manage the crisis in which they find themselves. The psychologist might teach brief coping techniques (eg, mindful breathing, problem-solving) or begin the process of establishing support outside of the hospital.

Clinical psychologists are also employable – there are frequent opportunities to develop one's career, and clinical psychologists are usually seen as an asset to a team. According to statistics from the CHPCCP website, 92 per cent of the trainees who completed training in 2018 were working as clinical psychologists (or at an equivalent level) within 12 months of graduating and 97 per cent of these were working in the NHS or other public sector. However, there are lots of people in this exact position (nearly 600 places are offered every year, with a completion rate of 99.4 per cent; CHPCCP, 2019) and – in any economy – job listings are not endless. The breadth of Clinical Psychology means that you can work in many different places: your training equips you to work

2.2: EXERCISE

Why do you want to be a clinical psychologist?

If you are considering a career in Clinical Psychology, have a think about why. Write down a few reasons why you want to be a clinical psychologist and compare them to those described above – and maybe others you might find elsewhere. Try to think about some of the more difficult aspects to the role – does this change your mind? Would another career be more appropriate? Are you fully informed about what it is that clinical psychologists do? Where do you see yourself working in ten, or even 20, years' time?

This can be a tough exercise, but it is worthwhile – it can save you a lot of time down the road.

across specialties (eg, children, addictions, medical psychology, learning disabilities) and to develop your interests further. By virtue of being a (clinical) psychologist, you will have established a good understanding of research, and might choose to pursue a more research-oriented path. Plenty of university professors have a background in Clinical Psychology.

If you speak to clinical psychologists, it is often the variety of the work that they enjoy above all. However, they will also comment (as seen in the case studies presented in this book) on the enjoyment of working with people, the changeability of the demands one faces, or the simple reward of helping others.

A TYPICAL DAY

A typical day in clinical practice might include meeting with others, including, but not limited to: nurses, occupational therapists, dietitians, paediatricians, psychiatrists, and other psychologists. One might conduct an assessment of a patient referred to the service and see two or three 'regular' patients, either side of eking out some time for lunch. In among all of that, there might be another meeting to attend, as well as the usual 'busy work' (screening referrals, liaising with GPs, writing letters). Although responsibilities of clinical psychologists vary, many view working directly with patients as one of their main roles; patients are at the heart of any service and, in many senses, are what the NHS is all about.

The development of clinical psychologists as providers of psychological therapy was, however, 'fraught with tensions' (Parry, 2015, p 181) and, although working with adults often dominates the narrative around clinical psychologists' work, this hasn't always been the case. As a clinical psychologist, one should consider all elements of the role – using continuing professional development (see Chapter 4) in order to remain competent and keep up-to-date. I know many clinical psychologists who shy away from ongoing research (perhaps an echo from the trauma of their dissertation), but it is important to make sure that you are in touch with the latest developments in your field. For me, I get this from research, attending conferences, and reading (journal articles, books, blogs, news articles, and so on), but there are other means.

As discussed in Chapter 1, the exact make-up of a psychologist's job will vary by grade and specialty. We will cover this a bit more in later chapters but will first cover the philosophy that underpins the approach of most applied psychologists, beginning with the application of evidence-based practice.

EVIDENCE-BASED PRACTICE

A feature of the clinical psychologist's approach that is often discussed is practising in an '*evidence-based*' manner: that is, '*the conscientious and judicious use of current best evidence in conjunction with clinical expertise and patient values to guide health care decisions*' (Titler, 2008). Although there has been debate around the merits of evidence-based practice (EBP), it underpins the professional approach of many clinical psychologists and more detailed discussion will be presented in Chapter 6. A similar model is that of the 'reflective scientist practitioner', which integrates the empiricism of EBP with the diversity of clinical presentations often seen.

Tension arises, however, within this apparently coherent model. On the one hand, EBP asserts that the most ethical way to treat patients is to use a treatment that has been reliably shown to have good effectiveness for their condition (akin in many ways to the 'medical model'). Much of the research in this area reports on evaluations of so-called 'treatment manuals'; that is, a codified means of providing treatment which can be a way of disseminating evidence-based treatments (EBTs). A more reflective approach (eg, Schön, 1983) advocates continuous learning in order to refine practice, and may be seen as being more 'person-centred'. In this philosophy, rigid adherence to manuals becomes an overly 'technological' approach (eg, Malatesta, 1995) and affords little room for individualisation. Furthermore, the classification of mental disorders is not without its critics, and comorbidity (where more than one psychiatric condition is present) is typically the norm. How, then, does one apply EBP with each patient?

The difficulty of when to rely on the evidence base and when to deviate can be clearly observed within the field of eating disorders. Best evidence for the treatment of bulimia nervosa (a relatively common eating disorder affecting around 1–2 per cent of Western populations) suggests that 40–60 per cent of people get better following cognitive behaviour therapy (CBT). This practice has been refined in recent decades and represents a significant improvement for an illness that was, until relatively recently, thought to be untreatable (see Jansen, 2001). However, basic mathematics will tell you that 40–60 per cent of people will *not* benefit fully from the leading evidence-based treatment. So, what is one to do? There is some evidence that another psychological treatment should be considered, but could it perhaps be the case that treatment for one of those 40–60 per cent needs to be individualised yet further?

Training in Clinical Psychology rarely includes explicit schooling on a certain manual or way of addressing a problem (which may be the case as a research psychologist working on a clinical trial, for example). By contrast, training reflects the duality of the reflective-scientist-practitioner model, preparing trainees to make informed decisions about healthcare while considering the 'best evidence' alongside the unique situation of the patient. Other careers in healthcare (see Chapter 8) deliver treatments more 'to the letter' and this might be an approach you prefer. Others are more 'patient-centred' and see the use of manuals as overly rigid and as minimising both the patient's involvement and the clinician's judgement.

2.3: RESEARCH SUMMARY

Use of manuals versus treatment 'as usual'

A research report appearing in the *International Journal of Eating Disorders* aimed to compare a manual-based approach to 'treatment as usual' (TAU) for adults suffering from eating disorders. The researchers randomised 71 patients to a form of CBT for eating disorders (CBT-E; Fairburn, 2008) and therapists were trained in this approach and received regular supervision from an expert in the treatment. A similar number of 72 patients received the TAU approach; this was based on CBT principles but could vary from weekly sessions to several group sessions a day for two to four days per week. The authors suggest that TAU '*is best described as more freely applied CBT compared to manual based CBT-E*'.

Around 18 months after the start of the study, the two groups (CBT-E and TAU) demonstrated few differences in outcomes. However, CBT-E (the treatment based on a manual) seemed to be associated with more rapid improvement and may require fewer session to demonstrate positive effects. Similar findings have emerged in other areas, such as psychological therapies for under-18s (eg, Weisz et al, 2006), although there have been critiques of these conclusions and more research is doubtless warranted (eg, Wampold et al, 2011).

Source: De Jong et al (2020)

This apparent tug-of-war between EBP and a more 'reflective' approach has been eloquently described in a number of articles (works by G T Wilson and Michael Addis are notable), with good arguments made for both 'sides'. How you choose to operate will eventually – as a clinical psychologist – be up to you (within the constraints of your employer, code of ethics, and so on), and most will always have their patient's best interests at heart. However, the absence of clear models for decision-making paired with the complexity of human psychology and behaviour represent an engaging challenge for those of us working in the helping professions. As a clinical psychologist, you can be at the forefront of treatment evolution – using your analytical skills to improve treatments and addressing (usually through empiricism) the key questions of what works for whom, and why.

FORMULATION

A related skill, not unique to the clinical psychologist but perhaps distinctive in its universality, is the practice of psychological formulation, which offers a helpful integration of EBP and reflexivity. Derived from comprehensive assessment and an understanding of human psychology and psychopathology, this is a means of developing an individualised portrait of the causal and maintaining factors in a given problem (such as depression, low self-confidence, grief, and so on). A good formulation highlights a patient's strengths and weaknesses, and gives that individual insight into why they behave the way they do. Different theoretical approaches (CBT, psychodynamic, etc) approach formulation in different ways and summarise it in different manners, but all will base any subsequent intervention on this 'psychological road map'. Formulations can be very simple or incredibly complex and can highlight one area of a patient's life, or attempt to summarise common patterns and pitfalls. A simple example of how thinking, emotions, and behaviour might interact in depression is shown in Figure 2.2. This model is typical of many approaches founded on cognitive behaviour therapy (CBT) principles.

An alternative exploration with this individual (looking more at behaviours that keep the cycle of depression going) might be summarised in the 'vicious flower', shown in

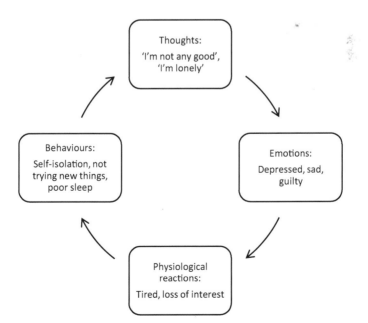

Figure 2.2 An example of typical symptoms in depression, and how thoughts, emotions, behaviours, and physiology interact.

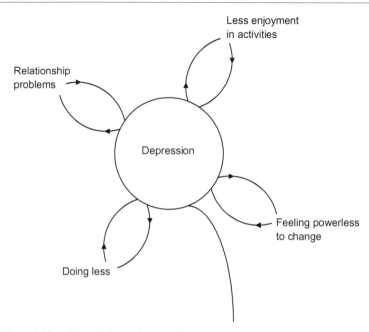

Figure 2.3 A 'vicious flower': how depression can be maintained.

Figure 2.3. Often, a synopsis is provided early on in treatment, written to the patient to summarise what has been discussed, and the shared view of their difficulties; the *formulation letter* (see Practice Summary 2.4).

A formulation can change over time (according to new information, changing circumstances, and so on) and, as such, evolves during treatment. It is used to guide treatment, which again highlights a potential conflict with an 'evidence base for an individual'; as Lucy Johnstone, clinical psychologist and staunch critic of the biomedical approach to psychiatry, notes, '*human emotional suffering does not come in neatly delineated categories*' (http://dxsummit.org/archives/1208). She has also espoused these ideas when working with teams trying to understand a patient's difficulties (see Johnstone and Dallos, 2014).

Formulation is a skill, like many others, that is taught and honed during the years before, during, and after formal Clinical Psychology training (the doctorate). It can be an excellent way of engaging with a patient and helping both of you make sense of why things are the way they are. Viewed through the lens of formulation, even the most incongruous of behaviours can be seen as a justifiable response to a difficult situation; a young woman who cries at the sight of a plate of food, or a middle-aged man who weeps with sadness at a picture of his daughter can both be understood by taking the time to discuss what thoughts and emotions they are experiencing. That is not to say that all patients will *want* to share this information with you or that they have the ability to insightfully describe their experiences, but therein lies the skill of developing a formulation.

2.4: PRACTICE SUMMARY

Part of a formulation letter

Dear Oliver,

Following our meeting last week, I am writing to summarise what you told me about your symptoms, and how they are working to keep things stuck – we call this a formulation.

You described that you often felt tired for no reason, and that you had lost interest in things you used to enjoy, such as playing football. You described feeling powerless to change this, and we discussed how you have become trapped in a 'vicious cycle' of being less active, and then being less inclined to do fun things, such as going out. We discussed how this makes you feel sad, but also guilty because you spend less time with your friends than you used to. You identified having negative thoughts about yourself, such as feeling lonely, that people don't like you, and that you are 'no good' at things.

Finally, we discussed how these thoughts, feelings, and behaviours are currently working against you – for example, by not feeling like you want to go out, you are spending less time with your friends, which is making you feel guilty.

I have seen formulations be incredibly powerful for patients and groups, but treatment is usually the next step in your journey with that person. Whole libraries have been written on psychotherapies, so I shall present only a flavour here of how clinical psychologists work therapeutically.

PSYCHOLOGICAL THERAPY

My own orientation lies pretty firmly within the overall framework of CBT – a therapy exemplifying the scientific approach to the understanding of psychopathology and its treatment. Although different variants exist, the central premise is that one's thoughts and behaviours influence each other and that, through focusing on the present (rather than the past), one can effect changes in thinking and behaviour that lead to desired outcomes.

A simple example can be extracted from the formulation described earlier in the chapter of an individual with depression, Oliver. Following a possible triggering event (which could be loss of a job), Oliver started to go out less (behaviour) and attributed this to his being a bad person (thought). One part of treatment might help Oliver see that going out less is contributing to his low mood, and aim to develop alternative thoughts, such as '*My friends would like to see me'.* A classic idiom that neatly describes the ethos of CBT is attributed to a Greek philosopher, Epictetus, who lived in the first century CE: *'Men are disturbed not by things, but by the view which they take of them.'*

Although CBT lies at the core of my experience (in large part, due to personal choice), training in Clinical Psychology also promotes exposure to different disciplines and approaches. I have worked alongside colleagues using systemic therapy, shared offices with practitioners of cognitive analytic therapy (CAT) and had supervisors who consider themselves strongly influenced by the psychodynamic tradition of Sigmund Freud, Melanie Klein, and others. Clinical Psychology equips you with the background to be able to make a choice about the therapeutic direction in which you may wish to go: if CAT floats your boat, you are well-positioned to consider further training and supervision; if you like CBT, you are probably well-versed in it and can polish your skills further over time. Providing interventions as a clinical psychologist will generally mean that you use one or two 'main' therapies but have the experience and knowledge to consider alternatives. If a client is struggling to make use of conventional CBT, you might consider supplementing your work with schema therapy (an integrative therapy), or through a greater focus on interpersonal relationships. Whichever approach resonates with you most, you will always carry the core principles of Clinical Psychology, such as the importance of psychological formulation and the reflective-scientist-practitioner model, with you.

2.5: REFLECTIVE SUMMARY

What does 'clinical psychologist' mean to you?

Write down a few ideas about what the phrase 'clinical psychologist' means to you. How would you describe what they do? What makes clinical psychologists different to other professionals, and what can they offer to teams in healthcare and beyond?

Your ideas might change as you read this book but, as you will see, the practice of a clinical psychologist is rarely static and will vary according to where one works.

FOLLOWING GUIDANCE

In the UK (and many other countries), there are sets of recommendations regarding which forms of psychological therapy to use, over how many sessions, and what to do if a treatment doesn't work. The National Institute for Health and Care Excellence (NICE) is one of the most influential bodies worldwide and provides recommendations for how to improve health and social care in the UK. As such, its remit is broad and includes many psychiatric conditions. Its clinical guidance is based on comprehensive reviews of evidence, but decisions are also based on judgements.

These guidelines are helpful – using the example above, adults with bulimia nervosa should be offered a CBT-based guided self-help programme as a first step. If this is unsuccessful or contraindicated, individual CBT should be considered. Beyond this, however, there is little additional guidance from NICE. Therefore, the skills of the clinical psychologist are essential here; using formulation and detailed psychological assessment, for instance, the psychologist can try to identify the best approach for an individual. More than guiding healthcare decisions, clinical psychologists can use their skills to develop novel treatments or evaluate those routinely provided in their services (commonly known as effectiveness studies). We shall return to the research role of the clinical psychologist in Chapter 6.

SUMMARY

This chapter will have helped you to think about what a clinical psychologist is, what they do, and whether you want to be one. It has touched on some of the key elements of Clinical Psychology and should have given you a sense of what it is to practise as a clinical psychologist. The next chapter therefore considers what routes exist to working as one.

REFERENCES

CHPCCP (2019, 1 September) Numbers. [online] Available at: www.leeds.ac.uk/chpccp/numbers.html (accessed 6 July 2020).

De Jong, M, et al (2020) Effectiveness of Enhanced Cognitive Behavior Therapy for Eating Disorders: A Randomized Controlled Trial. *International Journal of Eating Disorders*, 53(5): 717–27. [online] Available at: https://onlinelibrary.wiley.com/doi/full/10.1002/eat.23239 (accessed 6 July 2020).

Fairburn, C G (2008) *Cognitive Behaviour Therapy and Eating Disorders*. New York, NY: Guilford Press.

Good, B, Walsh, R M, Alexander, G and Moore, G (2014) Assessment of the Acute Psychiatric Patient in the Emergency Department: Legal Cases and Caveats. *Western Journal of Emergency Medicine*, 15: 312–17.

HMRC (2020) Percentile Points from 1 to 99 for Total Income Before and After Tax. [online] Available at: www.gov.uk/government/statistics/percentile-points-from-1-to-99-for-total-income-before-and-after-tax (accessed 6 July 2020).

Jansen, A (2001) Towards Effective Treatment of Eating Disorders: Nothing is as Practical as a Good Theory. *Behaviour Research and Therapy*, 39: 1007–22.

Johnstone, L and Dallos, R (2014) *Formulation in Psychology and Psychotherapy* (2nd ed). Hove, UK: Routledge.

Longwill, A (2015) Clinical Psychology Workforce Project Division of Clinical Psychology UK. [online] Available at: www.bps.org.uk/sites/www.bps.org.uk/files/Page%20-%20Files/Clinical%20Psychology%20Workforce%20Report%20%282015%29.pdf (accessed 6 July 2020).

Malatesta, V J (1995) Technological Behavior Therapy for Obsessive Compulsive Disorder: The Need for Adequate Case Formulation. *The Behavior Therapist*, 18: 88–9.

NHS Employers (2019) NHS Terms and Conditions of Service. [online] Available at: www.nhsemployers.org/pay-pensions-and-reward/agenda-for-change/nhs-terms-and-conditions-of-service-handbook (accessed 6 July 2020).

Parry, G (2015) Psychologists as Therapists: An Overview. In Hall, J, Pilgrim, D and Turpin, G (eds), *Clinical Psychology in Britain: Historical Perspectives* (pp 181–93). Leicester: BPS.

Schön, D A (1983) *The Reflective Practitioner: How Professionals Think In Action.* New York: Basic Books.

Scior, K, Bradley, C E, Potts, H W W, Woolf, K and Williams, A C (2014) What Predicts Performance During Clinical Psychology Training? *British Journal of Clinical Psychology*, 53: 194–212.

Titler, M G (2008) The Evidence for Evidence-Based Practice Implementation. In Hughes, R G (ed), *Patient Safety and Quality: An Evidence-Based Handbook for Nurses* (pp 1–47). Rockville, MD: Agency for Healthcare Research and Quality.

Wampold, B E, et al (2011) Evidence-Based Treatments for Depression and Anxiety Versus Treatment-as-Usual: A Meta-Analysis of Direct Comparisons. *Clinical Psychology Review*, *31*(8): 1304–12.

Weisz, J R, Jensen-Doss, A and Hawley, K M (2006) Evidence-Based Youth Psychotherapies Versus Usual Clinical Care: A Meta-Analysis of Direct Comparisons. *American Psychologist*, *61*(7): 671–89.

3 The route to Clinical Psychology and 'The Course'

In order to practise as a clinical psychologist in the UK and Ireland, one needs a further degree (currently doctorate-level) in Clinical Psychology. In addition, there is a formalised process for accreditation guided by specific standards and competencies that leads to professional registration as a practising psychologist. At present, following the three-year professional course, one is eligible for accreditation with professional associations, such as the Health and Care Professions Council (HCPC), British Psychological Society, or Psychological Society of Ireland. The Doctorate in Clinical Psychology (abbreviations include DClinPsych, DClinPsychol, ClinPsyD, and DPsychSc) forms the backbone of accreditation and is widely known simply as 'The Course'.

THE UK DOCTORATE IN CLINICAL PSYCHOLOGY

As mentioned in Chapter 1, the professional Doctorate in Clinical Psychology helps develop skills in clinical work, research, and leadership. This is usually achieved through a combination of university-based teaching and practical experience, drawing on a broad range of psychological models. Given the number of universities offering courses (see Figure 3.1), there is some variability in course content although many commonalities exist.

In the UK, these courses are currently funded by the NHS (with a similar arrangement covering part of the fees in Ireland), meaning that trainee clinical psychologists receive a salary for the duration of their course (in AfC parlance, at Band 6). Some self-funded options are available, but these are limited. However, it is unclear how long this situation will continue and reviews have been conducted by the UK Government with implications for the structure of training and funding (eg, NHS, 2016).

THE COURSE

The Doctorate in Clinical Psychology is what an aspiring clinical psychologist will typically aim to complete. In 2019, there were 30 training centres in the UK (based at universities; see Figure 3.1), offering 614 places (www.leeds.ac.uk/chpccp/). General criteria for consideration as a trainee clinical psychologist (your job title for the duration of The Course) include a good undergraduate degree (usually a first-class or 2:1) from a course that is accredited by the BPS (known as Graduate Basis for Chartered Membership), or from an

Figure 3.1 Doctorate in Clinical Psychology Courses in England, Wales, and Scotland.
Note: City of Lincoln denotes the Trent course (University of Lincoln and University of Nottingham). Data from CHPCCP (www.leeds.ac.uk/chpccp/).

1   University of Glasgow - "NHS Scotland"
2   University of Edinburgh - "NHS Scotland"
3   Newcastle University
4   Teesside University
5   Lancaster University
6   University of Leeds
7   Bangor University - North Wales
8   University of Liverpool
9   University of Manchester
10 University of Sheffield
11 Trent - Universities of Lincoln and Nottingham
12 Staffordshire University
13 University of Leicester
14 University of Birmingham
15 Coventry and Warwick
16 University of East Anglia

17 University of Essex (amended 18/10/19)
18 Oxford
19 University of Hertfordshire
20 South Wales
21 University of Bath
22 North Thames - University College London
23 University of East London
24 Royal Holloway - University of London
25 Institute of Psychiatry, Psychology and
    Neuroscience - King's College London
26 Salomons - Canterbury Christ Church University
27 Plymouth University
28 University of Exeter
29 University of Southampton
30 University of Surrey

equivalent 'conversion' course. This is built upon by relevant experience, often (although not exclusively) as a paid assistant psychologist. Individuals vary in their career histories leading up to The Course, so summarising a required – or even typical – route risks being misleading. Where I trained, my year group numbered 19 – two had PhDs (research degrees, both in a related field), one had a previous career in business, and a number of others had spent significant time outside of Clinical Psychology, deviating from the oft-assumed 'template'. The variety in this one cohort demonstrates that there is no single route into Clinical Psychology (discussed more in the next chapter) and, in my view, contributes to diversity within the profession. We even had one lecturer during our three years who held a triumvirate of doctorates – in Clinical Psychology, Medicine, and a PhD!

Figure 3.2 shows the structure of a stereotypical Doctorate in Clinical Psychology. Note that this is provided as an overview and will vary from course to course. Each programme adopts their own philosophy and unique take on Clinical Psychology, and will also have their own approach to teaching and learning. Similarly, some currently offer one placement in the final year whereas others provide two for each year of training. Some also offer part-time options although, at present, none can be completed by distance learning. Figure 3.2 is provided here to summarise a typical template for the three years of the doctorate, and more detail is available on each programme's website.

A proportion of trainee clinical psychologists have spent some time in research teams, usually in a clinically relevant setting (eg, a university department of Psychiatry) or researching an area with substantial clinical relevance. As with assistant psychologist positions, such roles tend to combine exposure to those affected by health problems, for example through assessing their eligibility for a treatment under study, with data analysis and other academic skills. They can be useful for building basic clinical skills (eg, assessment, engagement) while stressing the importance of evidence-based practice (see Chapters 2 and 6). As a result, individuals in such posts gain good exposure to many elements of Clinical Psychology, preparing them well for the professional doctorate.

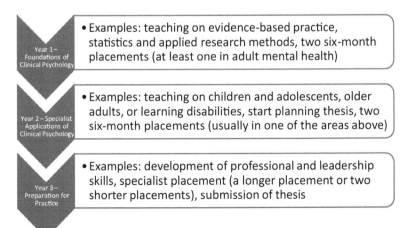

Figure 3.2 Overview of typical three years of study for the doctorate in Clinical Psychology.

My route was a simple one and, many might say, a serendipitous one. I duly completed my undergraduate degree and then proceeded to study for a Master's degree in research methods, with a focus on cognitive neuropsychology. Although my undergraduate degree classification was sufficient, looking back, I do feel that the extra knowledge gained during my Master's was helpful not only in getting on to The Course, but also in learning more about research methods, statistics, and suchlike. It was also fun.

During this year, I also volunteered as an assistant psychologist at a local Eating Disorders Service. I worked one-to-one using psychological approaches (doubting my ability to really help for the first few cases!), contributed to neuropsychological assessments, and did some work on an inpatient ward. It was the perfect complement to my academic studies, and also strengthened my CV for future roles. It also, perhaps most important of all, helped solidify the idea that applying what I knew about psychology to a real-world situation (particularly with people suffering from severe mental health problems) was what I wanted to do. It may seem that The Course requires you to have done a lot in order to be 'accepted' through its doors. While this may be true, it is also true that only experience will help you understand what you are applying for and what clinical psychologists do.

Having completed my Master's degree, I then worked as an assistant psychologist, in a paid role, in an NHS Child and Adolescent Mental Health Service (CAMHS). This was a great introduction to working with children as I saw conditions such as autism, selective mutism, attention deficit hyperactivity disorder (ADHD), social anxiety, and obsessive-compulsive disorder (OCD). I worked closely with psychiatrists and began to learn more about the role of education and how a psychologist fits within a multidisciplinary team (MDT). I also benefitted from some great supervision, and worked alongside some trainee clinical psychologists (who had 'made it'!) who also gave me some valuable advice and support. My supervisor and I got on well. He taught me important lessons, not only about Clinical Psychology, but also about working in the NHS as well as where work fits within one's life. He was relaxed and, in retrospect, indirectly helped me cope with the later demands of The Course.

'CORE COMPETENCIES' IN CLINICAL PSYCHOLOGY

Clinical psychologists are trained to work across levels of complexity, often employing different psychological models to work with both individuals and groups. As mentioned in Chapter 1, training is based on a number of 'core competencies', areas of activity that permeate all stages of a clinical psychologist's career. The nine core competencies of UK clinical psychologists are presented in Practice Summary 3.1.

When reviewing relevant experience, consideration of competencies is likely to be helpful. Trainee clinical psychologists (ie, those on accredited programmes) are expected to demonstrate that they can progress towards all of these competencies although, as might be expected in Clinical Psychology, development will continue throughout one's career. Experience gained prior to training is therefore of most relevance when it shows advancement of any of these core competencies, and this can be through research, clinical work, or any number of related roles. Most individuals begin to accrue experience in voluntary roles and we shall consider now the place of these within Clinical Psychology.

3.1: PRACTICE SUMMARY

Core competencies of clinical psychologists

1. Generalisable meta-competencies (eg, knowledge synthesis, 'using' the evidence base)
2. Psychological assessment
3. Psychological formulation
4. Psychological intervention
5. Evaluation
6. Research
7. Personal and professional skills and values
8. Communicating and teaching
9. Organisational and systemic influence and leadership

Source: BPS (2019)

'HONORARY' ROLES

As mentioned above, while studying for my Master's degree, I also held a voluntary (ie, unpaid) position as an honorary assistant psychologist. There has been some critical coverage about the exploitation of young graduates in so-called honorary posts (eg, www.mirror.co.uk/news/uk-news/graduates-told-work-free-year-6179446) and the relative merits are frequently debated in professional psychology periodicals and books. In my position at that time, I was fortunate to be able to manage this financially but took the role part-time and alongside my studies. In order to support myself financially, I took jobs that did not compete too heavily with these commitments, such as working in a bar. My supervisors were understanding and also very supportive, which helped a great deal.

Advantages of voluntary roles include their variety and the fact that they are fairly accessible; many charities and hospitals, for example, welcome volunteers and will provide on-the-job training as well as valuable experience. As a volunteer, you will typically have the opportunity to learn a lot about a given area, such as head injury, mental health, and so on, and other skills, such as interpersonal communication and teamwork, will also be developed as a result of such work.

Given that you are volunteering your time, it is reasonable to expect something in return, such as accruing worthwhile experience and perhaps opportunities to shadow other professionals. However, volunteers do not come at 'zero cost' to the provider; they incur expenses such as training, supervision, and investment in developing staff. While many volunteers are committed employees, some can cause issues for their host organisation which may be seen to outweigh their contribution. Volunteers are typically not bound under standard employment contracts and often leave posts at very short notice, potentially leading to gaps in care for patients or other service users.

Voluntary posts also offer another opportunity – that of contributing the skills you have developed during your Psychology degree to support the service. If you are working in a position like this, consider how you could use your analytical skills, or those with data management, to conduct a service evaluation, an audit, or a small piece of research.

It is important that you think carefully about any voluntary position, and it may be that – at least financially – this is not an option for you. Certainly, honorary positions have a place, but can risk exploitation of those with a 'do what it takes' attitude to get on in Clinical Psychology, and may also favour those in a position to accept a role that does not pay for one's time.

APPLICATIONS AND INTERVIEWING

A few months into my CAMHS job, I applied to The Course (more in hope than any real expectation) along with a friend of mine who was in a similar position. Each applicant can choose to apply to up to four individual courses located across the UK, with each course reviewing these applications to offer interviews and, ultimately, places. Some of these selection processes comprise a 45-minute interview, others are spread over two days with a mixture of interviews and group tasks. In our case, we were both amazed to be offered interviews, and I was offered only one from my four applications.

My interview was held in late April, and I felt incredibly lucky to have even been invited. The university staff were welcoming, and also operated a system whereby current trainees were around the waiting area to help you relax (as much as possible!) prior to your interview, and also to give you some informal information about The Course and life as a trainee clinical psychologist. From this moment, I knew I liked the university – it seemed relaxed but also professional and appeared to have student (trainee) welfare high on the agenda. These were qualities that mattered to me (and still do), but each course will have its own unique approach. The interview was good – I wouldn't necessarily say 'fun' but, contrasted with the experience referred to in Chapter 2, I felt that I came across well and that the interviewers seemed genuinely keen to know about me. It was later said to me that the courses aren't looking for a clinical psychologist – they want someone whom they can 'mould' and develop into a reflective, strong, and forward-thinking practitioner. I have met a number of individuals throughout my career who, prior to their interview for training, seem to believe that Clinical Psychology was their destiny. Interviewers usually comprise clinical psychologists, and they are pretty good at assessing individuals' motivations – they are looking for confidence, but also some humility. This can be a difficult balance to strike. Interviewers want you to be able to reflect on your experiences, but also to acknowledge where your weaknesses lie, and thus areas you might wish to develop during your three years of professional training.

Most trainees only get experience of one course at one university; I only had experience from one interview, and thus am partially sighted to the wider experiences of trainees at this, and other, stages of their careers. You will make your own journey through to Clinical Psychology (or another career, if you so choose), and my hope is that you will take some understanding from my experiences in order to prepare you for your own.

3.2: REFLECTIVE SUMMARY

Preparing for an interview

I often get asked how to best prepare for doctoral interviews. Although I do not currently sit on any admissions boards, I do have some bits of advice that you might find helpful if you have been invited to interview. For this exercise, consider asking yourself the following questions/prompts, but also consider others which might come up.

○ Why do you want to be a clinical psychologist?
This might seem like a silly question but, as well as being a straightforward 'ice-breaker', it can get to the heart of why you are applying.

○ What are some of the challenges of working within Clinical Psychology?
This is an opportunity to think a little about challenging cases but also how the skills of a clinical psychologist can be used to meet these challenges.

○ What theoretical models do you have experience with, and how might you develop these as a trainee clinical psychologist?
You may be familiar with common psychological approaches to mental health (eg, CBT) but also consider alternative psychological models – and don't be afraid if you have experience with something that is a little different!

○ Describe a recent research paper you have read and how it influenced your practice.
As with a number of skills we cover in this book, questions like this can help you think about the relevance of (academic) research to the 'real world'.

○ How have recent changes in the NHS changed the role of a clinical psychologist?
I found questions like this daunting at times. Try to remember that you won't be expected to have an encyclopaedic knowledge of the NHS but will be expected to have some understanding of how Clinical Psychology 'fits'.

○ Thinking about a particular patient you worked with, what did you learn from this, and what might you do differently as a result?
A number of questions will tap your reflective skills as well as asking you to talk about your clinical experience. Although this doesn't have to be copious, the DClin admissions criteria usually stipulate some contact with individuals in 'clinical' settings.

○ How do you cope with stressful situations?
This question will tell the interviewers a little about yourself, but will also give some insight into how you might cope with The Course (see also Research summary 7.1).

(continued)

As with many exercises, this is just a guide and should complement, not replace, otherwise thorough preparation. My main advice is to know about yourself and your work. For example, try to recall a piece of research you have done (eg, an undergraduate project) and be prepared to talk about it in some depth. Think about some patients with whom you have worked and remember what psychological models influenced your work.

STRUCTURE OF TRAINING

The Course itself is a blend of teaching, academic work (including research), and clinical practice (usually on placements lasting six to ten months). Each course has its own approach but, due to the formalised process for accreditation, they share many similarities. Placements give you an opportunity to learn about core areas of Clinical Psychology and are generally within NHS services, although occasionally can be provided by third-sector organisations or, sometimes, other Government departments. They are similar in many ways to assistant psychologist posts, although naturally involve a different level of working in the sense of greater degrees of responsibility and what is required of a trainee clinical psychologist. You will have a supervisor on each placement, and this responsibility is sometimes shared. Personally, I had a range of supervisors and most were excellent. All, however, shaped me as the psychologist I am now. I recall one in particular with whom I didn't 'gel' particularly well over the course of my six-month placement – his approach to psychological therapy didn't naturally match my own, and we didn't always agree on how we saw things. Nonetheless, the relationship was always respectful – particularly given my 'one-down' position – and it might have been easy for me to feel as though my supervisor was always right. Not once did I feel patronised, and I have later come to realise that many of his insights, while I might even now disagree with them, were incredibly valuable in their own way. Just as one size does not fit all for patients, so it is with our approach to the understanding of psychology and human behaviour. There are different strokes for different folks, as the idiom goes, and as clinical psychologists much of our appeal is the ability to take a meta-perspective – being able to 'see the wood for the trees' and take account of more than one viewpoint or school of thought.

Our course, in common with many others, was capped by a final placement that was both longer and more focused than the four that preceded it. It would be unfair to say that it was more difficult, but the extra time (eight or nine months compared to five or six) allows one to become immersed in that particular area and to have greater flexibility when working with patients. Mine was, perhaps predictably, within eating disorders, and the additional few months allowed me to implement treatment with a wider variety of patients than might have been possible in a shorter placement. Being just months from graduation, the level of clinical skill required is often expected to reflect that of qualified psychologists; again, this expectation adds pressure but also helps one develop. One of the most challenging aspects to this time, as I recall, was the idea that one would be 'qualified' in just a few weeks: the support of training, often seen as an encumbrance, would be gone and it felt, at more anxious times, as if one would be cast adrift. Some of these themes are also picked up by Jess, in the case study presented below. Jess recently qualified as a clinical psychologist and has written here about her experiences. Of course, the reality is far from this prediction – as a 'newly qualified' psychologist, others tend to respect that you may not have yet fully found your feet and that guidance is often required.

Case study 1 – Jess

Paul has kindly invited me to comment on life as a recent graduate of a Clinical Psychology doctorate to support this wonderful book. I am immediately noticing my difficulty in starting, and I attribute that to the fact that I am yet to integrate 'Doctor of Clinical Psychology' into my identity.

I have worked for more than a decade to reach this point and for the majority of that time becoming a clinical psychologist felt outside of my grasp because of the painful and exhausting application process. So many of us are capable of this role, yet very few of us are lucky enough to be offered a place on training. So for years I have protected myself from believing it was possible, while at the same time steadfastly knowing that it was.

Prior to starting my first qualified position, I went travelling for several months, to rebalance myself after three intensely challenging years. Training was all-consuming, despite me entering into it with relatively healthy boundaries and perspective; it demanded so much. Within three years of training you start five jobs that you didn't choose, in different teams and widely varying contexts. You embark on five new beginnings when everything feels unknown, from how to work the photocopier to, importantly, how to do the clinical work. You also experience five endings, with teams that you've become a part of, who have thoughtfully supported your development. Just as you feel like you might be capable of being a clinical psychologist, it is time to move on and start again. Alongside these professional challenges, you have a volume of academic work with doctoral-level expectations that place huge demands on your free time. And for all of us adult-learners, we have our other roles to fulfil, which for me included being a wife, a daughter, a sister, a friend. I was often left asking myself, in response to this menagerie of challenges, 'Can I do this?'

Now, seven months post-qualified, I did it and I am doing it! I am working for a service who offer specialist therapeutic interventions to adoptive children and their families. It is my dream job in a service with beautifully minded, intelligent clinicians who I am eager to learn from. I have a huge sense of pride in being able to occupy this role but the question of 'Can I do this?' still

(continued)

haunts me. The title alone seems to carry professional weight, with there being clear expectations that you are somebody who has worthy knowledge and whose input is valued. The reality is, I had one year of working in this specialism during training, and during that time my mind was distracted by my thesis and the other hurdles I had to jump to achieve my doctorate. My peers in other professions seem expert in their field but despite having worked for more than ten years, I feel like a novice in mine.

And then I am reminded of the compassion that we offer the people we support, taking a moment to reflect and turn this inwards. It is easy to make Clinical Psychology an intellectual exercise, feeling concerned about how much or how little one knows, being driven by a need to learn more. But that is assuming somewhat that our role is to impart knowledge, and my experience to date denies this. Ultimately, I believe it is our job to listen, really listen and hear. To bear witness to another's suffering, seeking to understand all that they bring, offering guidance at times, but most importantly, be a fellow human alongside them. And when it is stripped down that simply, I know that I can do that. Many people cannot because they are scared of what they will hear, they will want to solve the problem and offer solutions, it will feel too much to sit with the pain and discomfort. But as clinical psychologists we can be present in the darkness without needing to turn the light on.

As I bring this piece to a close, I am noticing my concern that I have not been specific enough about what a clinical psychologist is. I am asking myself questions such as, perhaps there is something different I could have written to be more helpful? Should I be more specific about my role? And this then makes me smile, is this not the mind of a clinical psychologist, always asking questions, seeking to know more, striving to do better, and ultimately caring about others with a desire to do your best by them?

KEEPING BALANCE

The Course was hard, no doubt about it, but some found it more bearable than others. I was able to find time for other things – sport was a big part of my life, and I joined a university sports team and met people whom I still count as good friends today. Social 'outings' to local watering holes were naturally a part of this, and the active and competitive nature of sport also allowed me to unwind in other ways. I have no doubt that this life beyond The Course helped me cope with the demands of being a trainee, and my advice to any Year 1 trainee is to make sure that you don't neglect other areas of your life. The Course can become all-consuming and, if you allow it to, can blind you to other experiences and opportunities that might actually improve your functioning as a clinical psychologist. I also made a core of good friends on The Course, who helped me put things in perspective and helped me through some of the more gruelling lecture days.

The academic element of the degree comprises a number of written assignments, such as case studies and small research projects. Some courses also have examinations. Perhaps primary among these is the dissertation – a large research project usually conceived at some time in the first year, and one of the last pieces of work to be submitted. Dissertations can include a number of investigative methods, including interviews (for example, with staff or patients) and large-scale questionnaire-based research projects. The choice of topic is ultimately up to the trainee, and you typically have both an academic and clinical supervisor to help you out. Our course was incredibly supportive and some of my academic support came from outside of the university. We were also afforded nearly three months of dedicated research time that can be used for data collection, and I used this to recruit students from another country in order to strengthen the scientific basis for my study and to conduct research in a culture different to my own. Following initial incredulity and perplexity from the course director, he had a 'go for it' attitude and allowed me to spend nearly two months of my studies abroad. Through this, I met many wonderful individuals with whom I now collaborate on research studies and other projects to this day.

The dissertation is finally evaluated through a viva voce examination (commonly referred to as a viva), as in other research degrees, such as PhDs. For the clinical doctorate, this typically involves being interviewed about your work by two examiners – one internal to the university, and one external. In order to aid my preparation, it was explained to me that I was the expert in this particular area (as I had spent two years all but immersed in the literature on the subject and had been responsible for every moment of the study's conduct) – but this did little to calm my nerves. The viva started well enough, with some 'introductory' questions that I handled fairly deftly. However, I began to be placed under greater pressure and found myself struggling with questions to which I wasn't sure I knew the 'right' answers. My external examiner launched a searching inquiry, and I recall noticing that the internal examiner showed a sense of empathy towards me. This tested my 'think on your feet' skills (to which I alluded earlier), and this experience – as my sweat-drenched shirt and nearly expired parking ticket would attest – was key in the development of later confidence in dealing with situations of uncertainty and where I might find myself being asked difficult questions. If this story sends a nervous shiver down your spine, you are not alone. The viva was all we could talk about in the weeks leading up to it, and few would look back and say they enjoyed it. Personally, I would say that I learned from it and, tough as it was, it certainly provided the makings for the development of internal strength and confidence that have been so important since.

That was my story (rather self-centred, for which I apologise). Other individuals whom I have met and worked with will have similar tales to tell, but the variety of these will demonstrate how there is no single road into Clinical Psychology. Some people have degrees in biology or classics and have done an accredited conversion course before pursuing relevant experience. Others have worked for years as an assistant psychologist (in one post, or a combination of many) and finally been given the chance to prove themselves on The Course. Others have worked in business before deciding that they want a career in the helping professions. All bring their own background and narratives to their work and, as mentioned earlier, are subsequently shaped in the crucible of clinical training.

Much as The Course is formalised, there are many opportunities within it. I had already established my foremost interest as eating disorders and was able to do a specialist (third-year) placement in this area. Other colleagues were interested in certain types of psychological therapy and pursued placements and supervisors where they could develop their passion. As we have seen, clinical psychologists work in many different areas and therefore individuals can choose to specialise at various points in their career (see Chapter 5).

TAKING THE QUALIFICATION ABROAD

A central theme of this book is the diversity and flexibility associated with a career in Clinical Psychology. As mentioned above, clinical psychologists can work with a wide variety of different groups within clinical settings, or move into research or teaching. Other clinical psychologists work as part of, or set up, an independent practice offering treatment, consultation, and so on. The strengths of Clinical Psychology (including, but not limited to, an evidence-based approach, rigorous training, and appreciation of individual differences) are consistent with the changing landscape of healthcare provision in the UK, and therefore mean that Clinical Psychology is likely to be crucial in the delivery of effective, equitable healthcare.

Obtaining recognition as a clinical psychologist in the UK is not necessarily sufficient to be able to practise abroad, but the quality and rigour of this training means that many will be successful in plying their trade outside of the UK. As we saw in Chapter 1, different countries will apply different licensing and training requirements, although some (eg, Australia; see Practice Summary 3.3) might be more accessible than others. If you think this might be an option for you, it is important to look at the licensing and registration requirements of where you intend to live, and that country's professional psychology body is a good place to start.

3.3: PRACTICE SUMMARY

Working abroad as a clinical psychologist

Working as a clinical psychologist in Australia can feel very different initially, due to the differences in training pathways and the healthcare system overall. Private healthcare is much more common and, if you have a diagnosed mental health problem, you are entitled to around ten subsidised therapy sessions per year. Many people prefer this option to Government-run mental health services, which means that plenty of work exists for private practitioners. It is not uncommon for clinical psychologists to set up their own private practice shortly after completing training. So, if you come to Australia to work as a clinical psychologist, you may also find yourself running a business too.

As for working in mental health and psychological therapy services, some offer Psychology-specific roles, which usually involve a combination of therapy and leadership responsibilities, while others will advertise general allied health positions, for which clinical psychologists can apply. The latter has pros and cons, of course. On the one hand, a clinical psychologist who has undergone extensive training in psychological theory and practice may feel somewhat 'de-specialised' working in these services, while on the other, they may have more opportunity for leadership due to this being the very nature of their core competencies.

As for Australia generally, working as a clinical psychologist certainly has its perks... such as practising self-care and having your lunch on the beach!

Some countries may have more relaxed criteria for the provision of psychological services, although it is likely that this will shift over time, as has been seen in the UK. Similarly, working in a research setting might be a way to get a job, and then develop the necessary licensing.

However, Clinical Psychology is not the only career for those looking to make a difference in healthcare. We will cover alternatives to Clinical Psychology and different career paths later, but the next chapter looks at what types of experience are of use early in one's career and how to make the most of them.

REFERENCES

BPS (2019) *Standards for the Accreditation of Doctoral Programmes in Clinical Psychology*. Leicester: BPS. [online] Available at: www.bps.org.uk/sites/www.bps.org.uk/files/Accreditation/Clinical%20Accreditation%20 Handbook%202019.pdf (accessed 6 July 2020).

NHS (2016) Review of Clinical and Educational Psychology Training Arrangements. [online] Available at: https://assets.publishing.service.gov.uk/government/uploads/system/uploads/attachment_data/file/510725/ Review_of_clinical_and_educational_psychology_training_arrangements_report.pdf (accessed 6 July 2020).

4 Beginning the journey to clinical psychologist

As detailed in the previous chapter, in order to train as a clinical psychologist in the UK one needs to complete the Doctorate in Clinical Psychology. Competition for places on the course is stiff and progression generally requires a mix of academic knowledge (supported by a good undergraduate degree) and relevant, paid experience. However, many individuals early in their career find themselves in something of a Catch-22: how do I get clinical experience when many jobs themselves require previous clinical experience?

STARTING OUT ON THE JOURNEY

My personal career began as an undergraduate studying Psychology. I was attracted to Clinical Psychology, and yet knew very little about it. A close friend on my course was also looking at this as a possible career and she was invaluable in steering me in the right direction as she had done enough research to know where to look next. My undergraduate thesis had a clinical element to it and, where possible, I chose modules that best reflected my strongest interests and the pursuit of a clinical career. I was an OK student – certainly not the brightest nor the hardest-working – but my grades on the clinically relevant modules were leagues above others in which I had, shall we say, a more tepid interest. I say this not to crow, but to illustrate another point for those considering a move in to Clinical Psychology: you do not have to be a genius (indeed, in some senses, it may be better if you are not), but you should get pretty good grades, or at least be prepared to work hard for them. Clinical Psychology is based on three central pillars – clinical work ('therapy'), academic understanding and research, and leadership.

I achieved a 'good enough' grade in my undergraduate course and then pursued a Master's that piqued my interest. As will be discussed in later chapters, there are many routes one can take prior to training as a clinical psychologist in the United Kingdom and mine was fairly orthodox – I got a degree, did further academic study, worked in a related field, and duly completed the Doctorate in Clinical Psychology. Knowing that the field of eating disorders was one within which I wanted to stay, I deliberately pursued post-qualification jobs in this area. I have worked primarily for the NHS during my career, but have also supplemented this through research, providing lectures, and working privately. I now find myself working full-time in academia, hoping to develop a clinically oriented research programme that can have a positive impact on those suffering from mental health problems and also bring on the next generation of clinical psychologists. This journey illustrates just some of the many paths a clinical psychologist can take.

The skills of clinical psychologists make them well-suited to working across a range of vocational settings. In healthcare, they work in both mental and physical health and apply psychological understanding to the assessment, evaluation, and treatment of illness and distress. Many of their skills are not unique, but the constellation of these attributes, paired with the rigorous training, makes clinical psychologists an asset across healthcare, health policy, research, organisation, and social care. The roles of clinical psychologists have been elaborated elsewhere (eg, Beinart et al, 2009; Carr, 2012) and can include working with expectant families, children, adults, and older adults. Many clinical psychologists also develop strengths in leadership and management, using their core training to offer clinical leadership as well as having influence in the development of care pathways from senior positions.

Development of these skills takes time; before choosing to read Psychology at university, I had considered Medicine. I thought at the time that I would end up in Psychiatry, so Clinical Psychology would be quicker (this was rather naïve, with hindsight) – as it happens, this was the right choice for me but one perhaps not made based on the best evidence! From finishing secondary school in the UK (usually aged 18), it can easily take eight to ten years to qualify as a clinical psychologist. Competition for this is stiff – of those

4.1: REFLECTIVE SUMMARY

Should I take time off?

Many individuals feel that getting on to training is singularly the most important goal and that doing so needs to happen quickly. There are two points about this which bear particular consideration. First, Clinical Psychology favours experience and so an application submitted soon after one's first degree is unlikely to be successful (although not impossible). Second, taking some time away might help you make a better-informed decision, perhaps with a stronger application.

Although other factors (eg, funding of training places) may be paramount in the decision to apply, it is worth considering whether you should take a break before pursuing Clinical Psychology training. As we saw in Chapter 3, many of my contemporaries had other careers before qualifying as clinical psychologists and many more took breaks, including gap years. Consider asking whether you feel ready for training or if you feel you need a break from education. This time away doesn't have to be 'wasted' – although even something like travelling might help your personal development and, ultimately, help you become a more rounded applicant and psychologist.

For an American perspective on this (which is nonetheless relevant), a 2017 article by Franz et al (see References) may be of interest.

applying for places on the professional Doctorate in Clinical Psychology, success rates over the past five years have been around 15 per cent (or one in every six or seven applicants). The level of that competition can also not easily be understated. I have previously reviewed applications for assistant psychologist jobs (typically a key step before applying to training) – in the most recent year, 51 applications were received within 24 hours of the post being advertised; all had good degrees and a strong academic record, the vast majority had clinical experience, and most produced well-written, erudite statements in their applications. The four or five individuals we interviewed each year who were unsuccessful all had relevant experience, a good degree (or two) and a strong desire to be a clinical psychologist. Of these many applicants, only one was offered the post.

WHAT SORT OF EXPERIENCE IS 'RELEVANT'?

Although students on the Course (typically referred to as trainee clinical psychologists) report a variety of previous experience, there tend to be some commonalities – and there are reasons for this. When undertaking a training programme as intensive and demanding as the Doctorate, it is important for students to be acutely aware of what will be expected of them. Clearly, there is a strong focus on acquisition of clinical skills and, while the Doctorate is designed to develop these to an advanced level, trainees will need to have demonstrated elementary abilities to show that they are capable of progressing further. Similarly, a good understanding of healthcare services and their (often complex) structures is another indicator that an individual is ready to progress to training, as is experience working with both psychologists and non-psychologists. Values and attitudes are important, too, as are wider 'professional' skills; needing to learn basic teamworking skills on placement, for example, will put additional pressure on both the trainee and the course.

Individuals early in their career will often bemoan the inescapable requirement for 'patient contact' to progress, often promoting a dichotomy that 'patients' are somehow different to the rest of the population. Although there are explicit characteristics that might define a certain patient group, there are many skills of a clinical psychologist which do not need to be honed exclusively in clinical environments. My first volunteer job was with a charity supporting survivors of brain injury and their families and carers. Although this is towards the more 'clinical' end of the experience spectrum, working with families (who could simply be defined as 'non-patients' using the dichotomy referred to above) was equally educational as any direct work with 'patients' and helped me develop skills such as communication, active listening, and discussing sensitive issues. Therefore, and as I often discuss with students, it is not the role per se that counts but what you take from it. Issues such as the quality of supervision, the skills you develop, and the ability to reflect on your experiences are key to an individual's development across different areas of competence (O'Shea and Byrne, 2011). That said, courses are probably looking for something more relevant than working in a supermarket (which is not to devalue this at all!) and so it is worthwhile looking for experiences that include an application of (Clinical) Psychology to show at least an appreciation of the usefulness of psychologically informed theories and knowledge.

Research experience is also important. It may be taken for granted that all of those eligible for Clinical Psychology training have conducted research in the past, usually as part of an undergraduate project. However, just as is the case with clinical skills, the quality of what was done will be far more illustrative of competence than the mere experience itself. I have seen examples of individuals who have become immersed in their research and used this to develop their skills, and others who have seen it as little more than a means of progressing through their degree. Given the academic demands of both Clinical Psychology training and further work in the field, it is important for applicants to demonstrate that they can meet the scholarly criteria of a doctoral degree and really understand the research with which they have been involved. Research also affords further opportunities for reflection and a consideration of the context within which clinical psychologists operate.

All applicants to doctoral courses will have an accredited degree (or equivalent) which has necessitated conduct of empirical research. In order to develop their skills, many candidates build on their research work through further academic study (eg, an MSc) or a job within a research environment. The more clinically related these experiences can be, all the better, and research skills are an important area of development for all clinical psychologists (covered later in Chapter 6), forming part of the core training competencies; as the BPS (2019, p 8) puts it, clinical psychologists are *'trained not only to be critical consumers of research, and ever emerging knowledge bases, but to contribute to this knowledge base through research, with relevant skills benchmarked at doctoral level'*. This parallels the clinical competencies inasmuch as there is an emphasis on self-reflection, personal and professional development, and a refined skillset that is a hallmark of the wider profession.

In summary, a good application need not provide evidence of proficiency in *every* area, but it will demonstrate potential to manage the academic demands of a doctoral training programme as well as showing insight into the clinical (and interpersonal) competencies required. Although some courses currently specify a minimum requirement for experience, the quality of that experience is equal to, and possibly more important than, the overall quantity. Given that many trainees will have had at least one unsuccessful application to The Course, patience is an important skill which, if not already learned, will have plenty of chances to develop.

A STRONG ACADEMIC BACKGROUND

Emerging research evidence seems to suggest that academic ability is one of the strongest predictors of both selection to the doctorate and later performance, albeit particularly in academic domains such as in-course exams (eg, Phillips et al, 2004; Scior et al, 2014). Given the limitations of this work, such as skewed samples, limited range, and oftentimes reliance on limited methods, findings should not be taken too far but do suggest that selection criteria are used by courses as proxies for the competencies required in later training (Phillips et al, 2004).

The majority of trainee clinical psychologists in the UK will have achieved a 'good' under-graduate degree (usually defined as a minimum of a 2:1). Anecdotal experience and some survey data (eg, O'Shea and Byrne, 2011) suggest that individuals who obtained a 2:2 degree classification can get on to training but need to supplement this with a further degree, such as a Master's. This may be seen by some as elitism but it is testament to the importance of the academic strength required when studying for a professional doctorate and many of the attributes necessary to practising as a clinical psychologist.

Other ways of demonstrating a strong academic background include having research work published and presenting at academic conferences. This can be difficult to achieve early in one's career for a number of reasons. For example, it is not uncommon for over a year to pass between completing a research study and eventual publication. Delays can occur following rejection from journals, time taken to peer review, and making corrections following editorial feedback. Although universities and academic staff are keen to support students to promote their research, there are many other demands on both parties' time which can make this seem easier than it is in reality. I regret not pursuing publication of my undergraduate research project but was lucky to see the product of my Master's degree in print. Therefore, my advice is to seek out opportunities (eg, conference presentations) – no matter how insignificant your work might seem – and also to ask academic staff if they need help in getting a paper together. Many academics have half-completed projects on their desk that need 'finishing' prior to sending to a journal and would welcome a talented student who is able to take the lead on data analysis and writing a draft, for example.

ETHICS AND VALUES

As we have seen, one of the core competencies of clinical psychologists identified by the BPS is that of 'personal and professional skills and values' and the HCPC also outlines an ethical framework within which those who are registered must operate. Abiding by a set of agreed principles is clearly not unique to Clinical Psychology but sound ethics and values are integral to safe and effective practice and therefore something that potential employers will be looking for applicants to evidence. Furthermore, psychologists are well-placed to reflect on ethical (or unethical) practice, considering the influence of social factors, issues of power, group dynamics, and so on. It is difficult to summarise what an 'ethical' practitioner looks like but consideration of diversity, understanding and applying ethical issues (eg, informed consent, confidentiality), and looking after oneself are all likely to feature, as well as understanding the limits of one's competence and demonstrating behaviour that upholds trust in the profession.

As with other areas of experience, it is not advisable to write on an application form that one has 'achieved' ethical practice but it is something that can be demonstrated in a number of different ways. For example, there might have been a time where you disagreed with someone but respected their viewpoint as coming from a different background to yours. Given the influence of context, it is not necessarily possible to say that one course

4.2: RESEARCH SUMMARY

Ethical development during Clinical Psychology training

A study of trainee clinical psychologists in the UK looked at their approaches to moral judgements, comparing first- and third-year doctoral students (Jenkin et al, 2019). The results indicated that all participants favoured an approach to moral decision-making that views rules as changeable and is based on a set of ideals as opposed to self-interest, for example. However, first-year students reported a stronger preference for this type of reasoning than third-year students. This could represent a regression, or simplification, in moral reasoning but might reflect a greater dependence on rule-based decision-making for the trainees in later stages. (It should also be noted the study was cross-sectional in design.) The authors recommend that training in Clinical Psychology should promote greater acceptance of the complexity of many professional dilemmas and that defaulting to a 'rule-following' culture should be discouraged.

Source: Jenkin et al (2019)

of action is right and another wrong (although there may be times where this is the case) and acting ethically amounts to more than following rules or imitating what others do. Therefore, training in psychology often has themes of ethics running through it and much of what is learned can only really be appreciated when applied to real-world situations.

Thus, ethical guidelines help psychologists in practice. For example, key principles around professionalism and confidentiality imply that clinical psychologists should keep appropriate records. Similarly, there may be times when adopting an ethical perspective will help guide difficult decisions. I have been present at many team meetings where there was no clear recommendation of how to proceed but that a view of what was 'the right thing to do' prevailed. The guidance of experienced colleagues is often paramount, but this is contingent on a sound relationship based on mutual respect. In many cases, psychologists are reminded of the importance of treating individuals as being of equal worth and not to discriminate based on characteristics such as age, ethnicity, sexual orientation, and so on. As we will see below, however, this is far from universally achieved.

HOW MUCH EXPERIENCE IS ENOUGH?

A frequent question concerns how much experience is necessary to get a job or get on to The Course and this, asked often in the early careers of aspiring clinical psychologists, cannot be answered simply. As suggested above, doctoral training programmes (and employers) will usually care more about what an individual has learned from their experience rather than how many years they have accumulated. Jobs – and that of a trainee clinical psychologist is no exception – will have criteria that they ask applicants to demonstrate (the 'person specification') but will also appraise this experience directly, typically through an interview. I have met with potential employees who excelled 'on paper' but struggled to communicate what they had learned and how they had developed as a result of these experiences at a subsequent interview.

It is common for applicants to Clinical Psychology training to have at least two years of paid experience in a clinical role, although this is a very rough figure and is highly variable (see, for example, O'Shea and Byrne, 2011). Some of this experience is as an assistant psychologist, whereas related jobs in healthcare can include working as a support worker, a healthcare assistant, or as an addictions worker. Similarly, roles in non-clinical environments, such as research assistants, can be important if they help you demonstrate commitment to and application of Clinical Psychology.

Experience goes beyond direct clinical work, and many roles offer opportunities to develop one's own knowledge. This is commonly known as continuing professional development (CPD), and is '*both a professional expectation and a personal responsibility for psychologists*' (BPS, 2012). CPD can comprise a range of activities but, in common with the approach of Clinical Psychology more generally, it is important to reflect on these activities and think about what you have learned, and how it can be applied. For example, you may wish to attend a conference but your reasons for doing so will be key to getting the most out of this. Are you attending a talk to enhance your knowledge of an area? Are you going to an interviewing skills workshop to develop your skills on questioning and eliciting information in clinical settings? How will the knowledge you've gained, and the experience of attending, influence your future practice? Thinking about questions like this can begin the process of reflection, deepening the impact of CPD.

It is important to get a mix of experience, in part as this shows that you are flexible enough to work in different environments, which can be used to demonstrate a breadth of knowledge. A CV showing two very similar jobs (eg, a support worker in a learning disabilities service, followed by an assistant psychologist job in the same service) is fine but you will likely need to show your ability to work in other areas to progress to clinical training. There will, of course, be exceptions to this but varied experience (probably with different services) is usually seen as a positive. However, as emphasised by organisations such as the BPS, it is not *just* the experience that is important but what you can take from it.

WHERE DO I START?

The good news is that you may have already made a good start and, in many cases, reading this book has shown some interest and ingenuity. If you've completed your undergraduate degree and have started accumulating experience, well done. If you're at an earlier stage in your career, use the advice presented here to shape your future to some extent and begin to think about where to invest your time (although consult other sources of information as well). If you're moving from another field, think about what knowledge you can bring, and how you can develop in areas where you might lack experience.

As mentioned earlier, there is some merit (and also some risk) in getting voluntary experience, which is typically easier to obtain than a paid role. Wherever you start, the role, where possible, should have some relevance to Clinical Psychology. However, gaining experience is not solely a means of bolstering your CV; it should be an opportunity to see whether this is something you would like to do for the rest of your working life.

Some individuals will begin accumulating experience during their undergraduate degree (and, in some cases, even sooner). Degrees that offer placements can be helpful as they will give support specific to these students and have formalised processes to ensure that the experience is generally relevant and meets an agreed set of learning outcomes. However, as this decision is usually made prior to starting university, it can feel like a big one to be making at a relatively early age. Nonetheless, spending a year 'in practice' during your degree (typically as a third year of four) can help develop skills and show these to future employers. Reflective Summary 4.3 summarises some ideas for gaining experience

4.3: REFLECTIVE SUMMARY

Gaining relevant experience

Undergraduate students might find it difficult to get paid roles working with a clinical psychologist, for example. However, there are several avenues to gaining experience that are relevant to Clinical Psychology. Some (but by no means all) include:

- contacting a local service (NHS, social care, private providers) to see if you can do some shadowing, even for a week or so;

- approaching charities to see if there is anything with which you can support;

- seeing if any schools can offer opportunities, particularly those who might be working with special educational needs as this might be more relevant;

- doing a placement over the summer – either locally or abroad (eg, with a voluntary organisation supporting vulnerable people overseas);

- gaining more experience in research – try to develop projects on which you have been working, or ask your project supervisor if there are any more opportunities;

- writing a study or paper up for publication in a journal.

Although 'starting early' is no bad thing (eg, see Knight, 2002, particularly Chapter 2), you shouldn't feel under too much pressure. In my experience, there is enough pressure to Clinical Psychology training without making students feel like there are countless peers who are constantly ahead of them – gaining more experience, working with patients, publishing papers. While there will be some individuals who are exceptionally motivated and (with some fortune) will have amassed significant experience, it does not mean that they have developed the 'right' skills from this experience. The journey to clinical psychologist is certainly a marathon rather than a sprint, and there will be plenty of opportunities for those who are keen and keep their eyes open.

Unfortunately, most undergraduate degrees in Psychology offer only limited exposure to Clinical Psychology, and therefore students only gain a nascent understanding of the field from lectures and assignments. However, this can be a good start to make you think about whether this is something about which you would like to know more, and could open doors to more significant experience (eg, volunteer work or a clinically related project). Some students will take degrees that offer more clinical experience, such as an integrated Master's or postgraduate study.

HOW TO STAND OUT

Given the competitive milieu of Clinical Psychology (see statistics earlier in this book and online at www.leeds.ac.uk/chpccp/numbers.html) it would be disingenuous to say that one does not need to stand out. However, in contrast to some of the sobering statistics in this area, diversity ought to be a strength of the profession and there might be many ways in which you can offer something unique. As noted above, there are commonalities in what is expected of trainees (and therefore the application requirements) but there are infinite ways of demonstrating this.

Going back to the idea that what one learns from experience is more important than the experience itself, think about what you have learned from your experiences so far (see Exercise 4.4). It might be that caring for a relative with dementia got you interested in the field and this was built on through your experiences as a support worker. You might have explored other career options only to return to Clinical Psychology, or taken a gap year that has furthered your interest in helping people. It is often difficult (and perhaps more so for those of us from the UK!) to 'sell ourselves' without feeling uncomfortable. Arrogance is a particularly unattractive trait when it comes to applying for Clinical Psychology training but it is important to ensure that you can give the best account of yourself.

The skills required of a clinical psychologist are varied, and there can be many ways of showing that you are capable of graduating into the profession. A sizeable minority of trainees will have had a previous career and 'made the jump' to Clinical Psychology; this experience is not wasted – the skills managing a busy professional kitchen, or looking after the needs of clients within an advertising service are relevant to the work of a clinical psychologist. When interviewing, for example, I am often fascinated when hearing about

4.4: EXERCISE

What makes you stand out?

Write down an experience you have had that might make you different from others in your position and think about it for a few minutes. This can be an incident that happened at work, an experience during a gap year, or something you did at school or university. What was good about it? What was less good about it? What was going on at the time which might have influenced how you responded? What did you learn from it? What can you learn from it now? Would it have affected someone else in the same way?

Short exercises like this can help develop reflective skills and demonstrate that most experiences have good and bad bits – and there is usually a lesson to be learned either way.

people's previous employment experiences outside of psychology and am intrigued to know what they can bring to our team. I met with a student considering a career in Clinical Psychology who had worked as a proofreader for a computer gaming company. We discussed how this experience – seemingly a virtual world away from Clinical Psychology – might enhance her academic writing and have developed her attention to detail and critical skills. Illustrating what has been argued in this chapter, it was perhaps not her work experience that was of most relevance, but what she had taken from it.

DIVERSITY IN CLINICAL PSYCHOLOGY

Diversity is key to the effective practice of Clinical Psychology, and yet it is only recently gaining more attention. A task force acting on behalf of the American Psychological Association argued more than 15 years ago that psychologists could do more to attract those from a variety of different backgrounds (APA, 2005). They highlighted specifically that psychology '*should not reflect the ills of society, but rather, be a model for what society should be – a place where diversity is mainstreamed and where mutual appreciation exists for the contributions of all*' (p 11).

The above quote highlights an important aspect to Clinical Psychology – that psychologists have a role in promoting inclusive practice and modelling appropriate conduct. It is regrettable that recent studies have suggested that the profession is underrepresented both in terms of ethnic minorities (eg, Callahan et al, 2018), men (Callahan et al, 2018), and people with disabilities (Andrews and Lund, 2015). It is not known whether other marginalised groups (eg, those of certain religious faiths) are also less likely to practise as psychologists, but it seems likely to be the case. Embedding diversity in Clinical Psychology training would be difficult to apply uniformly, influenced as it is by geographical, historical, and sociological factors as well as the many ways in which diversity is expressed (Hunsley and Lee, 2006). Nonetheless, greater training on diversity issues could not only improve competence but may help address some of the bias associated with understanding that is seen even within Clinical Psychology (eg, see Green et al, 2009).

If you are reading this book and feel that your diversity has been an impediment, Clinical Psychology offers a way of reflecting on that and, hopefully, turning it into a strength. As a profession, we have a responsibility to welcome diverse groups and to reflect the changing demographics in society. Further, the presence of multiple perspectives and opinions is likely to enrich our profession and move the field forwards. This is an area ripe for exploration and research and in need of champions to keep fighting bias and inequality.

STAYING UPBEAT

It will seem, at times, like the journey to Clinical Psychology is impossibly difficult. For some, this might be true and it may be worth considering a different way of finding career success (see, for example, Chapters 6 and 8). However, with patience, perseverance, and perhaps some optimism, the right opportunity will present itself and you want to ensure that you are in the best position to make the most of it. This is made easier if, for example, you are able to travel independently or are unencumbered by the pressures of childcare or mortgage repayments. Unfortunately, the nature of Clinical Psychology selection may have resulted in a bias towards certain groups, although there are schemes to redress this imbalance (eg, Cape et al, 2008).

If you feel that Clinical Psychology is the right career for you and, importantly, that you can add something to this profession that others might not, then do keep going. There are many positive stories of people who have worked incredibly hard to get onto The Course and subsequently relished being a part of it. Use others to support you – be that family and friends or others in a similar position to you whom you might never have met in person; having people who know little of the pressures can be as useful as having people who know them all too well.

Ultimately, if Clinical Psychology is to continue as a respected, even revered, profession, then competition for places will persist. It might even be the case that the standards required of applicants, in a Darwinian sort of way, ensure that the profession stays strong in the face of wider pressures, such as cuts to health services and the changing landscape of healthcare. We will discuss ways in which the field of Clinical Psychology might change over time in Chapter 9 but now move on to consider whether, as a clinical psychologist, one might choose to specialise or not.

REFERENCES

American Psychological Association (2005) APA Presidential Task Force on Enhancing Diversity: Final Report. [online] Available at: www.apa.org/pi/oema/resources/taskforce-report.pdf (accessed 6 July 2020).

Andrews, E E and Lund, E M (2015) Disability in Psychology Training: Where Are We? *Training and Education in Professional Psychology*, 9: 210–16.

Beinart, H, Kennedy, P and Llewelyn, S (2009) *Clinical Psychology in Practice*. Chichester: Wiley-Blackwell.

BPS (2012) *Continuing Professional Development Policy*. Leicester, UK: BPS. [online] Available at: www.bps. org.uk/sites/www.bps.org.uk/files/Professional%20Development/CPD%20Policy.pdf (accessed 6 July 2020).

BPS (2019) *Standards for the Accreditation of Doctoral Programmes in Clinical Psychology*. Leicester, UK: BPS. [online] Available at: www.bps.org.uk/sites/www.bps.org.uk/files/Accreditation/Clinical%20 Accreditation%20Handbook%202019.pdf (accessed 6 July 2020).

Callahan, J L, Smotherman, J M, Dziurzynski, K E, Love, P K, Kilmer, E D, Niemann, Y F and Ruggero, C J (2018) Diversity in the Professional Psychology Training-to-Workforce Pipeline: Results from Doctoral Psychology Student Population Data. *Training and Education in Professional Psychology*, 12: 273–85.

Cape, J, Roth, A, Scior, K, Thompson, M, Heneage, C and Du Plessis, D (2008) Increasing Diversity Within Clinical Psychology: The London Initiative. *Clinical Psychology Forum*, 190: 7–10.

Carr, A (2012) *Clinical Psychology: An Introduction*. Hove, UK: Routledge.

Franz, M R, et al (2017) Taking a Gap Year: A Guide for Prospective Clinical Psychology PhD Students. *The Behavior Therapist*, 40(6): 212–17.

Green, D, Callands, T A, Radcliffe, A M, Luebbe, A M and Klonoff, E A (2009) Clinical Psychology Students' Perceptions of Diversity Training: A Study of Exposure and Satisfaction. *Journal of Clinical Psychology*, 65(10): 1056–70.

Hunsley, J and Lee, C M (2006) *Introduction to Clinical Psychology*. Mississauga, Ontario: John Wiley & Sons.

Jenkin, A C, et al (2019) Moral Judgments and Ethical Constructs in Clinical Psychology Doctoral Students. *Ethics and Behavior*. DOI: 10.1080/10508422.2019.1684294.

Knight, A (2002) *How to Become a Clinical Psychologist: Getting a Foot in the Door*. London: Taylor & Francis.

O'Shea, G and Byrne, M (2011) A Profile of Entrants to Irish Clinical Training Programmes. *The Irish Psychologist*, 37(5): 118–23.

Phillips, A, Hatton, C and Gray, I (2004) Factors Predicting the Short-Listing and Selection of Trainee Clinical Psychologists: A Prospective National Cohort Study. *Clinical Psychology and Psychotherapy*, 11(2): 111–25.

Scior, K, Bradley, C E, Potts, H W W, Woolf, K and Williams, A C (2014) What Predicts Performance During Clinical Psychology Training? *British Journal of Clinical Psychology*, 53: 194–212.

5 To specialise or not to specialise?

I first knew I wanted to be a clinical psychologist when I was 18 or 19, although it is possible that a desire to work in the field of mental health was present before that. Since that time, however, most of my clinical practice and nearly all of my research has been focused on helping people with eating disorders. These illnesses directly affect around 5 per cent of the adult population (although disordered eating behaviours affect many more) and are characterised by disturbances in eating behaviour, seen alongside specific psychopathology (disordered thinking) such as preoccupation with food and excessive concerns about weight and shape. I have found it to be a challenging and hugely rewarding field in which to work.

When I get asked how I got into eating disorders, the answer I often give (when I am forced to be brief!) is that I attended an undergraduate lecture that seized my interest and it hasn't let go since. I usually add that I can rarely countenance my working in another area of mental or physical health. However, this almost myopic passion has perhaps come at a price.

A TRADE-OFF

Due in large part to the wide scope of Clinical Psychology, it is inevitable that one will be faced with a number of decisions about one's career. The choice of specialising is one of those, as it frequently involves achieving a balance between competing, and often incompatible, aims. Within the Improving Access to Psychological Therapies (IAPT) programme, for example, commissioning arrangements mean that adults with depression and anxiety are usually the focus of treatment efforts. Although some areas of the UK have expanded this service (seeing long-term physical health problems, for instance), it is rare that a practitioner will come in to contact with a patient who reports, for example, delusions that the Government is following them as their primary complaint. Such individuals may be assessed but quickly referred to other (usually specialist) services that are more suitable for their needs. To take that example further, an individual with such delusions may be seen within a service offering Early Intervention for Psychosis (EIP), where practitioners (including clinical psychologists) will see few patients for whom psychosis is *not* one of their key symptoms.

As we will review in greater detail later in this chapter, different (sub-)specialisms appeal to different individuals. For example, some areas are more predictable in terms of their job demands (such as working hours or even salary), whereas others might appeal on a

5.1: EXERCISE

What is your motivation?

Spend a few moments thinking about whether you want to work in a specific area of applied psychology. If you feel that you don't have a specific interest (such as learning disabilities or forensic services), think about whether you would want to work in physical or mental health, or perhaps even healthcare generally. If you're not really sure, just try to go with an idea – you don't have to stick with this for your whole career!

Once you have an idea about what area you would like to work in, ask yourself why. What is it that attracts you to it? What do you find interesting? What might you find difficult? Do you have any experience (either personal or professional) to draw on? Finally, do you think this might change? If not, perhaps challenge yourself to have another area about which you might like to learn more.

more personal level – such as choosing to work with older adults having had a grandparent with dementia. Variety is one reason many people choose Clinical Psychology and working in more 'generic' services (such as Adult Mental Health Teams or many Child and Adolescent Mental Health Services) often entails contact with people affected by different psychiatric disorders on a daily basis. It is not that eating disorders or other specialisms (such as, for example, learning disabilities or forensic services) are monotonous – far from it! – but they do necessarily constrain the work one does to a certain extent. Such a situation therefore begs the question 'Should I specialise, or not?'

TYPES OF SPECIALISM

Although Clinical Psychology is itself a branch of applied psychology, a number of specialisms have emerged within the field itself (see also Research Summary 1.1 on page 5). As the profession and wider healthcare environment evolve, these areas may develop in tandem (Forensic Clinical Psychology is not considered above, for example) and generate further sub-specialties. As we will discuss further in this chapter, many clinical psychologists work generically and serve clients with a wide range of different needs, whereas others occupy roles within highly specialist areas.

The result has been that clinical psychologists are seen across several areas of mental and physical health, contributing their unique skillset to improve the lives of patients. Many roles and responsibilities that the clinical psychologist has in one area (whether generic or specialist) will not differ substantially from those of others working elsewhere.

Core skills – such as establishing and developing relationships with others, psychological assessment and formulation, delivering psychological interventions, and so on – are seen across disciplines although their application and the nature of the patients may differ.

It should be noted that, while the emphasis here is on healthcare, clinical psychologists can be seen in other settings. The training is such that the skills of a clinical psychologist can be of use to any number of different organisations. Although some of these skills, such as establishing relationships, oral communication, and testing hypotheses, may not be unique to clinical psychologists, their background in psychology and models of human behaviour means that they often make effective organisational leaders.

SPECIALISM IN TRAINING

In the UK and Ireland, Clinical Psychology training is probably best considered as 'generic' in that it provides prospective clinical psychologists with a wide range of skills and experience to prepare them for later practice in a number of areas. Although many courses will offer the opportunity to experience a more focused application of training within a 'specialist' placement, the overall curriculum reflects the intent to provide psychological intervention to any client group (McPherson, 1992).

Where I trained, we were offered a choice of placements in our third year. Options included working within a 'generic' service, such as Adult Mental Health, with a focus on a particular therapeutic approach that was not part of core training, or specialist areas, such as (spoiler alert!) eating disorders.

During the first two years of the course, I had received some, albeit limited, experience working with disordered eating; this had merely whetted my appetite to do more and I was lucky enough to secure my final placement in an adult eating disorders service. This placement built on the core training in Clinical Psychology and developed my knowledge and understanding of eating disorders. For example, I was exposed to the unique challenges of working with eating disorder patients and the specialist knowledge that is often required in the earliest meetings with patients and families. Due to the significant physical comorbidities seen in eating disorders, for instance, it is imperative that clinical psychologists have a rudimentary understanding of the physical risks which can arise – an area that would not usually be covered in core training or other areas of mental health.

The 'physical' side of eating disorders is always present when working in this area and I have seldom seen the connection between mind and body so clearly as when working with people with disordered eating. Luckily for me, I have been well supported by other professionals (such as nurses, dietitians, and more senior psychologists) and it was always stressed that one should not exceed one's competencies (relating to some of the ethical principles and values of psychologists discussed in Chapter 4). However, developing a basic understanding of issues such as medical risk assessment (including when to ask for advice) was something that can only be learned on a specialist placement with appropriate support. Similarly, the psychological therapy I learned on this placement (a form of cognitive behaviour therapy for eating disorders) is one that I still practise today, and in which I supervise others.

Although training across a breadth of experience is good preparation for later work, there are advantages to developing specialist knowledge early in one's post-qualification career. For example, working within a specialism allows one to develop a very specific skillset and immerse oneself in a given area. For me, it turned out to be an area in which I still work now and continue to develop my understanding and abilities. In the case study below, Georgina talks about working in a specialist Clinical Health Psychology setting, and how some skills learned working in mental health have been useful, whereas it has been important to develop others uniquely suited to the particularly challenges of working in physical health.

 Case study 2 – Georgina

Having spent most of my career as a Clinical Psychologist in mental health, making the move to a physical health setting felt like a big change. In reality, there were probably more overlaps than differences, but the predominant use of medical terminology is something I am still getting used to two years down the line. I work in Respiratory Medicine, primarily with patients diagnosed with the hereditary condition cystic fibrosis (CF). At any one time we have around 380 patients, many of whom will be under our service for life, so therapeutic relationships are often formed and grow intermittently and at a slower pace over a number of years. This is very different to the traditional pathway of referral-treat-discharge I experienced in mental health services.

Psychological services in physical health are often set up and organised in different ways. Some psychologists are employed directly by, and embedded within, their specialist teams. Others are based in psychology departments, running outpatient clinics and/or feeding into different wards and specialties as and when needed. I imagine there are a few psychologists working somewhere in between. Both systems have their benefits and challenges. I am based on a hospital ward with a multidisciplinary team, including medics, physiotherapists, dietitians, specialist CF nurses, and ward nurses. The opportunities to learn about other professions, their roles and how they contribute to the wider picture of patient care are endless and for me this is one of the biggest draws to this area of work. Having a team around me who know the patient (and often their families) well can also be a really helpful source of information and provides a different insight.

The challenges are that I can feel on my own a little with only a few people around who speak the same psychological 'language' and that, with only a handful of psychologists employed within the Trust, our professional identity and value can feel a bit lost at times.

My role

Most people will go through challenges in life that impact their emotional well-being. For individuals with CF, this will also include the challenge of living with a progressive health condition that requires time-consuming treatments and is likely to significantly reduce quality of life and shorten life expectancy. These factors contribute to the higher rates of depression and anxiety in patients with CF. Broadly, my role is to help patients recognise the factors contributing to their emotional distress and help them identify and put in place strategies that will help get them out of the cycles they feel stuck in. Everyone is different, but some of the typical themes I work with include:

○ ***Treatment compliance:*** *Treatment for CF is time-consuming, with patients often reporting that it gets in the way of living a 'normal' life. However, poor treatment compliance is likely to result in lung function deteriorating faster. In turn, this can impact quality of life and may prematurely limit their capacity to work, engage in social activities, and affect relationships. The interaction between these biopsychosocial factors can create a self-maintaining cycle. However, supporting patients to improve treatment compliance is an important part of breaking the cycle.*

○ ***Adjusting to loss:*** *The recent introduction of new medications targeting a genetic defect in CF is providing new hope for patients. However, life expectancy is still comparatively low – at just under 50 years. The impact of this can be widespread and will affect the decisions patients make throughout their lives regarding work choices, relationships, and children. These, combined with changes in functioning over the years, can mean themes around loss and adjustment are often a focus.*

○ ***End of life:*** *Personally, this is probably the most emotionally challenging part of my role. Patients at the end of life often need the time and space to think about the themes this generates. Whether this is about reflecting on the lives they've led, the conversations they want to have with loved ones, or the memories they want to leave for their children and families. It's an important process that can help both the patient and family when death is inevitable.*

(continued)

There are a number of psychological models that have been shown to be helpful for patients with physical health difficulties, including cognitive behavioural therapy (CBT), motivational interviewing (MI) and acceptance and commitment therapy (ACT). The model of working you choose will depend on a number of factors, including the nature of the difficulty, patient characteristics – such as previous experiences of therapy and preferences – and NICE guidelines. However, I have always felt that the overarching priority is to develop a way of communicating with your patient in a way they connect with.

Alongside this, a significant part of my role is about helping staff to understand our patient group from a psychological perspective. Supporting the team to develop their own skills in formulating the behaviours they observe or manage any rifts or relational issues is important and can contribute to the patient's approach to CF care. The aim is to help the team explore different ways of working and/or communicating with patients, especially when having difficult conversations and can help build communication and trust over time. This is done through regular reflective practice groups, teaching, and one-to-one discussions.

My experience of working in a physical health setting has been broad and varied. In contrast to many specialist services, patients will often bring a range of difficulties, including depression, addictions, relationship and adjustment issues at varying levels of severity and chronicity. The issues aren't always mental health, but often more related to emotional well-being, which can lead to small packages of work that can make a real difference, through to longer-term therapy. Having the opportunity to work with individuals during some of the most challenging and emotive periods of their lives is a privilege but is also emotionally demanding and has again highlighted the importance of developing good self-care strategies. A lot of the themes described here around treatment compliance, adjustment, and loss are relevant to a range of areas of clinical health and clinical psychologists can often be found in a range of services, including cancer teams, pain management, and brittle asthma to name but a few. For me this is one of the attractions as the opportunities for varied and rewarding work are endless.

FURTHER TRAINING

As is evident from the examples provided in this book, a clinical psychologist's development continues in many forms beyond completion of the doctorate. This can be relatively 'informal' (eg, reflecting on one's own practice) or can involve attendance at academic conferences or other forms of professional development (see also Chapter 4). However, some specialties require additional formalised education – either as relatively short courses (perhaps five days) or longer, practical training.

One example of the latter concerns individuals who wish to practise as clinical neuro-psychologists. In the UK, entry to the Specialist Register of Clinical Neuropsychologists requires a minimum of two years of structured supervised practice (or the part-time equivalent) and, similar to the Doctorate in Clinical Psychology, is delivered through a partnership of higher education institutions and NHS Trusts. Training as either a clinical or educational psychologist (for the paediatric route) is typically required, and the advanced course can lead to specialist knowledge of neurological conditions, psychological assessment, the effects of brain damage, and so on.

Clinical neuropsychology is not unique in this respect. There are many other avenues for further training open to clinical psychologists, and the profession – given its grounding in psychological assessment, formulation, and multiple psychological therapies – prepares students well for learning about more advanced areas. This diversity and evolution of Clinical Psychology can come at a cost, however, and one example of this is the issue of role blurring.

ROLE BLURRING

In the context of modern healthcare, the growth of Clinical Psychology has been associated with an expansion of the roles clinical psychologists are expected to perform. Whereas clinical psychologists may have historically been part of an *'ancillary service to the medical profession, operating in very confined contexts'* (MAS, 1989), the role today encompasses a much wider remit and has also fostered greater autonomy for practitioners. One of the main shifts has been from a primarily clinical responsibility (psychological assessment and provision of psychological treatment) to one where clinical psychologists play a greater part in organisation and management. While such expansion is likely to enhance the standing of the profession, many see this progression as an example of 'role blurring', a concept that has been hotly debated due to its potential for adding confusion and ambiguity but also encouraging flexibility and a patient-centred approach (eg, see Brown et al, 2000).

The reorganisation of (mental) healthcare since the late 1980s has challenged stereotypical professional roles, and thus the concept of role blurring is not confined to one profession. In addition to being subject to these changes, psychologists have been part of the argument for less clearly demarcated boundaries, developing the concept of 'boundary spanning' in the 1970s (eg, Adams, 1976) and studying behaviour between groups to reduce threat and associated biases which may occur during organisational change (eg, Rosenthal and Crisp, 2006).

One effect of role blurring (see Practice Summary 5.2) that has been suggested is that practitioners can experience role confusion, with group functioning ultimately being impaired (Brown et al, 2000). Further, performing tasks outside of one's core practice might result in a loss of efficiency (although the reverse might also be true). At least one author has suggested that role blurring is exacerbated by a '*stick-together-to-survive*' mentality (Mair, 1996, p 504), such that holding tightly to one's profession may risk ostracism from one's team.

5.2: PRACTICE SUMMARY

Claiming new territory: An example from the medical field

Despite sharing the goal of providing the best care for patients, there have existed tensions between healthcare groups with one oft-cited example that of the relationship between doctors and nurses (eg, Salvage and Smith, 2000; Snelgrove and Hughes, 2000). In the UK, there has been a growing trend for nurses to perform tasks that were historically the preserve of doctors in an effort to improve quality and increase capacity (Rashid, 2010). However, within this change there has been an argument that nursing has '*lost its way*' (Salvage and Smith, 2000). Commenting on the resultant confusion, Salvage and Smith (2000) summarised the position as follows:

> *Nurses, more assertive, educated, and competent than ever before, resent what they see as continuing putdowns by a profession holding all the cards. Doctors, puzzled and unaccustomed to being challenged, are themselves resentful at the apparent undervaluing of their competence, knowledge, and skill by nurses, the public, and policymakers.*

Although systematic reviews have generally supported the idea that nurse-led care has a positive effect on patient satisfaction, the number of hospital admissions, and mortality (Martínez-González et al, 2014), role changes have been associated with reduced job satisfaction in the context of performance targets and compromised professional values.

Conversely, '*creeping genericism*' in healthcare (Brown et al, 2000) has been recast as a positive feature of teams, seeing permeable boundaries as progressive and leading to a more flexible service for patients. Initiatives to promote shared, or multidisciplinary, working have been promoted by a succession of UK governments and also represent an international trend (Nasir et al, 2013). For example, the integration of mental health and social services aims to reduce discontinuity between services, thereby minimising patient distress and confusion and addressing poor interdisciplinary communication, co-ordination, and decision-making (Belling et al, 2011).

Whether role blurring is positive, negative, or, more likely, a mixture of both, it has become a salient issue for many healthcare professionals. It may be more likely in settings where demand is high, or where specialist skills are scarce (such as rural areas). Clinical psychologists are not immune from these pressures, which may drive burnout and affect healthcare professionals' ability to perform their jobs, but they can also be part of initiatives to drive improvements and increase efficiency throughout services. There is perhaps an onus on the clinical psychologist working in these teams to apply their skills and knowledge to ease these pressures. While responsibility cannot be laid only at the clinical psychologist's feet, the profession has always been one to adapt and innovate and, through so doing, support the wider infrastructure and create space for reflection and considered thought.

PROS AND CONS

As touched on throughout this chapter, there are a number of pros and cons to specialising within one area of Clinical Psychology, such as learning disabilities or trauma. I summarise these in Table 5.1, principally as a prompt for further thought, as there are likely to be many more reasons beyond this; some might seem contradictory but are likely to depend on individual circumstances. Ultimately, the decision whether to specialise may not be yours to make – it could be dictated by job availability, location, or other factors that are outside of your control. Therefore, as in many areas of this book, the idea of

Table 5.1 Some pros and cons of specialising within Clinical Psychology

Pros	Cons
Enables one to feel truly immersed in a given area	Puts constraints on decisions later on in one's career
Affords easier continuity in one's role – seeing patients with similar presentations across posts	Tied to one type of service (eg, there is rarely more than one eating disorders service in a UK county, and sometimes not this many)
One can become a 'master of one trade'	May be difficult to 'change back' having worked in one area for a long time
Greater opportunity for jobs and career progression given fewer individuals who are 'expert' in a given specialism	Greater competition for jobs as fewer roles exist (see *pro* opposite)
	Less room for expansion, such as learning new therapies or approaches

specialising is presented to illustrate some aspects to life working as a clinical psychologist to be considered as opposed to something that must be decided upon in advance of pursuing one's career.

As mentioned above, Table 5.1 is provided principally as a stimulus for reflection and consideration, and perhaps should be taken with a pinch of salt as it is likely to reflect my own biases about specialisation. Many Clinical Psychology graduates will not have the choice of whether to specialise, but I would advise not considering this too early in your career (and, yes, I am aware of the overt hypocrisy in that statement!). Clinical training does a wonderful job of exposing trainees to a diverse array of people and problems, but openness at this stage (and even earlier) will likely pay dividends later on. However, if you are lucky enough to find a niche about which you are truly passionate, this may provide the foundations of a long and happy career.

SUMMARY

This chapter has introduced some of the benefits and challenges of specialising as a clinical psychologist. For myself, and given the option, I would choose working with eating disorders again and again. Others are happier seeing a wider variety of clinical presentations, and many others enjoy the challenges of moving between different areas. Having written this chapter and reflected on its content, I think so-called 'specialist' and 'generic' services are almost certainly more alike than they are different.

If you have chosen to work in a helping profession, and Clinical Psychology in particular, you are likely to have developed several personal traits and skills that will be useful throughout your career. Whichever service you work in, the fundamentals are generally the same – we do our best to help patients, using the evidence where we can, and are guided by our training and ethical practice at all times. Although I have worked in the field of eating disorders almost exclusively for over a decade, I consider myself principally a clinical psychologist – and as a clinical psychologist, I am privileged to belong to a highly trained and dedicated family who appreciate the strength of difference alongside the bonds of familiarity. As Dr Bennet Omalu, forensic pathologist (and the first individual to identify and describe Chronic Traumatic Encephalopathy [CTE] as a disease in sportsmen, www.ucdmc.ucdavis.edu/pathology/our_team/faculty/OmaluB.html), said 'what binds us together is far greater than what separates us'. I see this as entirely relevant if you are considering a decision about choosing a path within Clinical Psychology.

One area perhaps conspicuously absent from this chapter has been whether to specialise as a researcher, clinician, or perhaps both. As this relates strongly to the central pillars of Clinical Psychology discussed in Chapter 4, the following chapter relates wholly to the role of the clinical psychologist as both researcher and clinician.

REFERENCES

Adams, J S (1976) The Structure and Dynamics of Behaviour in Organizational Boundary Roles. In Dunette, M (ed), *Handbook of Industrial and Organizational Psychology*. Chicago: Rand McNally.

Belling, R, et al (2011) Achieving Continuity of Care: Facilitators and Barriers in Community Mental Health Teams. *Implementation Science*, 6: 23.

Brown, B, Crawford, P and Darongkamas, J (2000) Blurred Roles and Permeable Boundaries: The Experience of Multidisciplinary Working in Community Mental Health. *Health and Social Care in the Community 8*(6): 425–35.

Mair, P (1996) Psychology in the Australian Outback: Rural Health Services. In Martin, P R and Birnbrauer, J S (eds), *Clinical Psychology: Profession and Practice in Australia* (pp 480–507). Melbourne: Macmillan Education.

Management Advisory Service to the NHS (MAS) (1989) *Review of Clinical Psychology Services*. [online] Available at: www.mas.org.uk/uploads/articles/MAS%20Review%201989.pdf (accessed 6 July 2020).

Martínez-González, N A, Djalali, S, Tandjung, R, Huber-Geismann, F, Markun, S, Wensing, M and Rosemann, T (2014) Substitution of Physicians by Nurses in Primary Care: A Systematic Review and Meta-Analysis. *BMC Health Services Research*, 14: 214.

McPherson, F M (1992) Clinical Psychology Training in Europe. *British Journal of Clinical Psychology*, 31: 419–28.

Nasir, L, Robert, G, Fischer, M, Norman, I, Murrells, T and Schofield, P (2013) Facilitating Knowledge Exchange Between Health-Care Sectors, Organisations and Professions: A Longitudinal Mixed-Methods Study of Boundary-Spanning Processes and their Impact on Health-Care Quality. *Health Services and Delivery Research*, 1(7). [online] Available at: http://eureka.sbs.ox.ac.uk/4866/1/Nasir_et_al_%282013%29_Facilitating_knowledge_exchange.pdf (accessed 6 July 2020).

Rashid, C (2010) Benefits and Limitations of Nurses Taking On Aspects of the Clinical Role of Doctors in Primary Care: Integrative Literature Review. *Journal of Advanced Nursing*, 66(8): 1658–70.

Rosenthal, H E S and Crisp, R J (2006) Reducing Stereotype Threat by Blurring Intergroup Boundaries. *Personality and Social Psychology Bulletin*, 32(4), 501–11.

Salvage, J and Smith, R (2000) Doctors and Nurses: Doing it Differently: The Time is Ripe for a Major Reconstruction. *BMJ*, 320(7241): 1019–20.

Snelgrove, S and Hughes, D (2000) Interprofessional Relations between Doctors and Nurses: Perspectives from South Wales. *Journal of Advanced Nursing*, 31(3): 661–7.

6 Research in Clinical Psychology

As we saw in Chapter 1, the origins of Clinical Psychology can be traced back to the late nineteenth century. However, the discipline began to take shape in 1949, when a group of psychologists and other professionals, including psychiatrists, social workers, and nurses, gathered in Boulder, Colorado, to discuss standards for doctoral training in Psychology.

One important outcome of this conference (and perhaps a rarity in that participants reached consensus on the issue!) was that clinical psychologists should be trained as both researchers and clinicians. Despite some objections to the notion of this model – for example, that interests in research and clinical work are incompatible – the 'scientist-practitioner model' was largely supported and has since been widely promoted within Clinical Psychology. What follows is a consideration of this approach within modern Clinical Psychology, and then a review of the extent to which research impacts the day-to-day practice of a typical clinical psychologist.

THE SCIENTIST-PRACTITIONER IN CLINICAL PSYCHOLOGY

As touched on throughout this book, there is a contradiction in modern Clinical Psychology: despite the Boulder model (the 'scientist-practitioner approach') asserting that professional psychologists should engage with both research and clinical roles, a large proportion of clinical psychologists have published either one or no research articles. Some authors have questioned the viability of the scientist-practitioner model; some years ago, Cohen (1979, p 780), for example, concluded that 'professional practice appears to be little influenced by mental health research findings', and subsequent research with other practitioners has supported Cohen's viewpoint (eg, Morrow-Bradley and Elliott, 1986). Rather than explicitly consulting research studies in a given area, many therapists (not necessarily clinical psychologists) who participated in these studies reported that clinical experience (such as working with patients and discussion with colleagues) was their most useful source of information about psychotherapy.

Reflecting on clinical experience and consulting research articles or attending academic conferences need not be mutually exclusive, however, and the 'scientist' part of a scientist-practitioner can also be satisfied through evaluating one's own interventions and generating research outputs, as we shall see below.

EVIDENCE-BASED TREATMENT AND CLINICAL PSYCHOLOGY

One of the most common terms heard within Clinical Psychology, 'evidence-based' can be a contentious term. Generally synonymous with 'empirically supported', questions have been raised about what this really means. How much evidence is needed for a treatment to be 'evidence-based'? Of what quality should this evidence be? What if there exists little – or no – evidence? How do we know that we have access to *all* of the evidence?

Evidence-based treatments are those '*interventions or techniques (e.g., cognitive therapy for depression, exposure therapy for anxiety) that have produced therapeutic change in controlled trials*' (Kazdin, 2008, p 147). Evidence-based practice, therefore, is broader and represents '*the integration of the best available research with clinical expertise in the context of patient characteristics, culture and preferences*' (APA, 2006, p 273). This approach has been formalised, to some extent, within the establishment and remit of the National Institute for Health and Care Excellence (NICE), an independent body which aims to '*improve outcomes for people using the NHS and other public health and social care services*' (NICE, 2020). NICE produces guidance informed by current evidence and publishes guidelines and quality standards related to particular areas of health and social care.

Clinical psychologists have occupied positions as ardent champions of this approach while also offering searching questions of how the scientific application of research findings (particularly within the 'randomised controlled trial') can be faithfully adopted in a field as dynamic, and at times complex, as mental health (see, for example, Salkovskis, 2002). The views of clinical psychologists were captured in a recent study, summarised in Research Summary 6.1.

6.1: RESEARCH SUMMARY

Clinical psychologists' views on guidelines

A study published in 2017 looked at UK clinical psychologists' views about the NICE guidelines. The authors interviewed 11 clinical psychologists from a variety of settings and at different levels of seniority and asked them to share their thoughts about NICE guidelines.

The study revealed mixed views among the participants. The guidelines were seen as a '*useful guide to the evidence base*' (Court et al, 2017, p 902) and as a tool which could be used to promote consistency and as a means of improving access for those experiencing mental health problems. However, the guidelines were also seen as creating '*an illusion of neatness*' (p 902) not matching everyday practice in clinical environments. This perception led to some practitioners using the guidance flexibly (eg, using them as guidelines rather than '*somebody telling me what to do*' [Participant Kim, p 905]), some reported ignoring them, whereas others felt compelled to conceal details of their practice from managers, whom they felt to be applying pressure to be 'NICE-compliant' (ironically, something which the early proponents of evidence-based practice warned against).

Influencing this, the authors suggested, were the clinicians' beliefs about what Clinical Psychology is and that guidelines which endorse the '*reification of psychiatric categories*' (p 906) could devalue clinical psychologists' contribution and steamroll over their unique skillset. The study illustrates many of the pressures in modern healthcare and how this might sit (sometimes uneasily) alongside the philosophy of Clinical Psychology.

Source: Court et al (2017)

The idea that these two things can be integrated does not come easily to many (see also Blaine, nd) but neither individual clinical expertise nor the best available external evidence is enough on their own (Sackett et al, 1996). A move to balance clinical expertise and 'best' evidence was heralded in the early days of defining evidence-based practice (Evidence-Based Medicine Working Group, 1992; Sackett et al, 1996) but an evidence-based stance has sometimes been mistaken to mean a 'cookbook' approach to clinical care. Within Clinical Psychology, there has been widespread doubt about the relevance of evidence-based practice, and therefore some resistance to its adoption (Lilienfeld et al, 2013b). However, such resistance '*may inadvertently fuel the continued popularity of unscientific or even pseudoscientific interventions*' (Lilienfeld et al, 2013b, p 884) thus harming both patients and the profession of Clinical Psychology. It is therefore important to consider the role of scientific understanding within Clinical Psychology, and the role that clinical psychologists play in the move towards effective, evidence-based healthcare.

WHY IS SCIENTIFIC RESEARCH UNDERUSED IN CLINICAL PSYCHOLOGY?

A full review is outside the scope of this chapter, but it is important to touch on the issues around scientific practice in Clinical Psychology given that this is not only debated at policy level but is also likely to inform your own view of treatment and day-to-day practice. Furthermore, as we see a rising influence of evidence-based practices in healthcare, the clinical psychologist can have an important role in translating research to practice, and vice versa.

Several studies have highlighted that only a minority of clinical psychologists regularly engage in the production of research, resulting in discussions about why this might be so. Oftentimes, clinicians (ie, those who work predominantly in clinical settings) see much research as neither applicable nor relevant to everyday practice. At the same time, researchers (ie, those who work predominantly in academic settings, and often not directly with patients) claim that many studies conducted in 'routine' clinical settings are not of sufficient methodological quality, and can therefore contribute only a small amount (if at all) to the advancement of knowledge.

Parts of this argument may seem fussy or of minor significance, but these issues often strike at the heart of what it is to practise as a clinical psychologist. For example, if you consider evidence-based treatments as a *sine qua non* of clinical work, you may have particular ideas about how treatment manuals should be used in your practice. By contrast, if you see these manuals as overly prescriptive and having been developed from populations that do not resemble the people whom you see every day, your attitude may be one that favours a more intuitive approach. I have faced this tension when providing and receiving supervision (how closely does one stick to a manual when providing psychological therapy?), introducing new treatments to a service, working with patients who do not 'fit' the model, and innumerable other scenarios.

One pre-eminent scholar in this field succinctly summarised the status quo: that some areas of clinical practice display '*an indifference to scientific research... [and] others an outright antipathy*' (Lilienfeld, 2010, p 283). Aside from confusion regarding one's own professional identity, this conflict can have more practical implications. For example, in one study, one in five therapists surveyed reported never having studied a specific treatment manual for eating disorders (Tobin et al, 2007) and another study found that only a small number of clinicians reported using techniques '*that underpin and define*' a specific eating disorder therapy (Waller et al, 2012, p 174). Surveys of sufferers and their families echo these findings; one study of parents of children with autism found that many were regularly using treatments that lack strong empirical support, leading the authors to conclude that '*the presence or absence of empirical evidence did not differentiate between commonly used and rarely used treatments*' (Green et al, 2006, p 81). Given that the role of clinical psychologists is to educate as well as treat, as a profession we need to be doing a better job of getting effective treatments to those with health problems.

6.2: EXERCISE

Appraising the evidence

Take a moment and think about what evidence-based practice means to you. If you were treating someone with a health problem (or, indeed, being treated yourself), what would you want to know about the treatment? Would you be convinced by a large, group trial or would you want to know more about the individuals in this treatment?

When you read a research study, do you look elsewhere to confirm its findings? What sources would you consider 'reliable'? What would you do if there was no evidence?

USE OF 'MANUALISED' TREATMENT

It is clear that, across many illnesses and presentations, effective treatments exist. Given that, in addition to demonstrated efficacy (eg, within a research study), treatments have often been additionally supported by expert consensus, it has led some to conclude that *'the burden of proof rests with practitioners'* who depart from using these techniques (Lilienfeld et al, 2013a, p 388), which are often delineated in manual form.

Many therapists might object to the idea of manualised treatments on the basis that their experience tells them what they need to know (findings from studies like that of Tobin et al, 2007, seem to suggest that this is indeed the case). However, these decisions are liable to be influenced by thinking biases and distorted perceptions, ultimately leading to decisions based on a partially obscured view of current evidence. I have probably met with hundreds of patients through my work and it would be impossible to remember the specifics of each one's outcome, particularly those methods or techniques that were particularly effective (or ineffective). If this seems defensive, consider how many variables one might need to review in order to assess the best course of treatment for a given patient. The therapist must discount those variables that will not impact outcome (probably an impossible task itself) and then consider the remainder in their decision-making before reaching a conclusion and proceeding (Kazdin, 2008).

As a further example, humans are prone to apply biases in their thinking and the practice of psychotherapy is no different. Glenn Waller, a clinical psychologist based in the UK, has suggested that such biases cause therapists to attribute 'failed' cases to patient characteristics and be less likely to consider their own role in the process, which can have important implications for longer-term outcomes. However, to be aware of biases is not to discount the intuition of a trained practitioner. As Monte Shapiro, one of the pioneers of Clinical Psychology in the UK, remarked in 1967, *'energy and enthusiasm do not... have to be maintained by unvalidated beliefs'* (p 1042) and it should be pointed out that following a guideline *too* rigidly can also reflect poor clinical practice (Parry et al, 2003).

6.3: PRACTICE SUMMARY

Biases in the therapy room

Most of us know what a 'bias' is (defined by the Oxford English Dictionary as: *'An inclination, leaning, tendency, bent; a preponderating disposition or propensity; predisposition towards; predilection; prejudice'*), and many of us might be aware of some of our own. To think that psychological therapists have prejudices may seem disagreeable but psychologists and therapists, like all humans, are subject to biases. Biases help us process the world around us, using 'shortcuts' to process complex tasks in order to make judgements (Tversky and Kahneman, 1974). For example, it would take an exceptional memory to remember every object that we

(continued)

saw in a room, so our brain filters out some of these objects and 'remembers' only the most important ones (to try this, make a list of all the objects on your kitchen countertops, and then go in to see if you missed any).

A therapist's bias might include cultural beliefs shared with many people (eg, beliefs about 'typical' families or those of a certain weight status) as well as others that are more specific to the clinical psychologist's work. For example, Walfish and colleagues (2012) surveyed 129 mental health professionals and asked them to rate their skills relative to other therapists. Their results were suggestive of a 'self-assessment bias', whereby clinicians overestimated their abilities relative to their peers, with none rating their clinical skills below average. (In case you think this might be unique to therapists, similar results have been found in engineers, software developers, and naval officers; for a review, see Dunning et al, 2004.)

It is unreasonable, therefore, to expect therapists (like anyone else) to show *no* bias, but it is important to be aware of biases and, as a clinical psychologist, to reflect on these (eg, in supervision) and use alternative approaches, such as consideration of outcome data, to ensure they don't cloud one's judgement too much.

Wider issues also have an impact on this debate. For example, despite many Clinical Psychology courses producing 'scientist-practitioners', there remains something of a career split between these two camps. Clinicians tend to follow a patient-facing route (working in the NHS or in private practice) with researchers staying in a more academic environment, leading psychologists 'to be characterized by the scientific or the applied tradition, and [leading] their professional lives accordingly' (Frank, 1984, p 420).

Many clinical psychologists, however, do straddle this divide. Aside from those who consider themselves scientist-practitioners, many professionals have so-called 'split posts', whereby they work for part of their week in an academic department and the remainder in a patient-facing role. Similarly, some clinical psychologists will be involved with clinical research through academic clinics, typically based within universities and often funded by research organisations or charities. These clinics deliver treatments to patients with diagnosed conditions, although it has been suggested that therapists in research clinics may have smaller caseloads and receive more supervision than clinicians in other healthcare settings (Southam-Gerow et al, 2003), adding fuel to the argument that these situations are not representative of the 'real world'.

Finally, one might also consider ethical issues pertinent to this debate. For example, is it ethical to provide a treatment that has not been studied in an area where there are established therapies with a strong evidence base? When we are giving advice about another person's health, life, or career, is it ethical to base these on our own gut feeling or experience? When considering allocating a clinician's time to research, to what extent can this be afforded in the context of long waiting lists? To return to Shapiro's (1967) views, the clinical psychologist 'has a responsibility to the community to see that substantial amounts of public money are only spent on procedures which are justified by the current stage of knowledge' (p 1042).

GETTING THE FULL PICTURE

Overlooking – or misunderstanding – evidence can have grim consequences. For example, reboxetine is a medication used in the treatment of depression. Given initial reports suggestive of efficacy, reboxetine was recommended in a number of practice guidelines and was endorsed by the Medicines and Healthcare Products Regulatory Agency (MHRA), a body that regulates medicines (and related areas, such as medical devices) in the UK. Following this early promise, a group of researchers in Germany decided to look at all of the available studies comparing reboxetine to either a placebo or another antidepressant drug (Eyding et al, 2010). These researchers used a technique known as meta-analysis, whereby the results of different studies are collated and combined to draw conclusions about effectiveness that would not be possible in a single trial. They looked at data from both published sources (eg, scientific journals) and that of trials detailed elsewhere (eg, by contacting the manufacturer for unpublished data). When all of these studies (13 trials including more than 4,000 patients) were considered together, it was concluded that reboxetine was *'an ineffective and potentially harmful antidepressant'* (Eyding et al, 2010, p 816). However, others have since critiqued this review, including the MHRA, who concluded that *'overall the balance of benefits and risks for reboxetine remains positive'* (MHRA, 2011; see also Cipriani et al, 2018).

So, where does this leave us? The case of reboxetine is more complex than the paragraph above can communicate (although similar cases exist, such as the use of the antidepressant paroxetine for children and Tamiflu© in the treatment of influenza) and it should be noted that no legal transgressions have been recorded relating to the use of reboxetine. However, awareness of the complexity around an evidence base can paint a confusing picture. For example, it is likely that the effect of a drug, say, will vary according to treatment setting (eg, inpatient or outpatient) and the severity of the illness of each patient. One can imagine that, with a psychological treatment, the number of variables influencing a patient's outcome may be even greater. The answer, then, is not to reject all knowledge on the assumption that it is flawed, but to systematically review the best available evidence to drive optimal decision-making. This can feel overwhelming but leads to the conclusion that psychologists need to embrace *'a multidimensional conceptualization of evidence'* which takes account of issues such as methodological rigor, how 'recovery' is defined, and how treatments might achieve their effects (Lilienfeld, 2019, p 246). The nature of training leaves clinical psychologists well-placed to make evidence-based decisions and apply their knowledge of both psychological therapy and rigorous research methods to determine the most appropriate treatment approach for their patients.

In the 1980s, it was argued that psychotherapy research needed to move beyond traditional methods of experimental psychology, reflecting the complexity and diversity seen in psychotherapy. A number of authors (see, for example, Kazdin, 2008) have offered cogent suggestions for bridging the research–practice divide. I do not profess to offer a solution to the ongoing controversy resulting from the Boulder Model, but find it hard to dispute the position of eminent American psychologist Paul Meehl, as cited in Peterson (2000), who said that *'Clinical Psychology is an applied science, therefore partly an art'*. (I am not breaking too many taboos in my support of Meehl; those who had the privilege of speaking with him universally described him as the smartest psychologist, perhaps individual, they had ever met.)

I was recently revising the content of a module taught to undergraduate Psychology students and had cause to reflect on this topic. It is my belief that providing the best service to patients involves the artistic application of current understanding. For instance, using treatment manuals in one's practice is not simply a case of regurgitating hackneyed anecdotes or tried-and-tested behavioural experiments; rather, it involves judicious use of effective treatment techniques, tailored to the unique presentation of each individual (see also Rosen and Davison, 2003). The clinical psychologist should be deeply conversant with treatments and be able to apply them in a flexible way that is true to both the documented effectiveness of the intervention and the individual needs of the patient. By doing so, we can hope to remain faithful to the founding principles of evidence-based psychotherapy, and to *'identify and apply the most efficacious interventions to maximise the quality and quantity of life for individual patients'* (Sackett et al, 1996, p 72).

HOW EMBEDDED IS SCIENCE IN MODERN CLINICAL PSYCHOLOGY?

The Boulder Model has informed current 'core competencies' of clinical psychologists, such as conducting research and devising, modifying, and evaluating practice to improve outcomes. Therefore, even if clinical psychologists do not routinely publish research studies, consideration of scientific principles is likely to inform their approach to their work.

Although the pressures of working in healthcare can often lead to prioritising clinical need, use of research to improve health is explicitly enshrined in the NHS constitution, wedding public healthcare to evidence-based practice. This relationship with evidence-based practice is also emphasised through the association between healthcare providers and non-governmental public bodies, such as the National Institute for Health and Care Excellence (NICE). These bodies base guidance on the best available evidence, typically conducting and commissioning reviews of published literature alongside input from experts and the lay public. This guidance then informs how healthcare is delivered, including recommendations for different mental and physical health conditions. Other factors, however, seemingly complicate the conduct of high-quality, psychological therapy research, such as the move in some countries to fund biomedical research over intervention studies (Insel, 2015) and these too will have a bearing on the evolution of evidence-based treatments and their use.

When considering the use of 'scientific evidence' in Clinical Psychology and all of its complexities, it might be worth considering what the field would look like if there were no evaluated criteria for decision-making (Kendall, 1998). It is likely to be at the detriment of the field more widely and could lead to poorer care for patients – the very thing that we all (researchers and clinicians alike) strive to avoid.

ENGAGING WITH RESEARCH AT THE INDIVIDUAL (CLINICIAN) LEVEL

If this myriad of issues seems overwhelming, do not panic. One does not have to be Paul Meehl to contribute to useful research that advances the provision of healthcare. Small steps in moving the discipline forwards can sometimes be as significant as huge trials, revolutionary theories, or great technological leaps. Karl Popper (1970, p 54) gives the example of there being '*hardly a less revolutionary science than descriptive botany*' but that the descriptive botanist contributes strongly to the field at large through addressing problems of description, species differentiation, and disease characteristics. In Popper's view, progress in science is characterised by knowing more than we did before.

George Stricker (eg, 2007) has operationalised this approach within psychotherapy as the Local Clinical Scientist (LCS) model, referring to practitioners who integrate knowledge and theory within a context of scientific questioning. If this seems familiar, the LCS approach has echoes in the practice of many areas of Clinical Psychology. For example, the CBT approach to evaluating the veracity of thoughts relies on a method whereby thoughts are elicited (eg, '*If I go to a busy restaurant, I'll have a panic attack*') and subsequently tested in a methodical and explicit manner, through so-called 'behavioural experiments' (eg, see Bennett-Levy et al, 2004).

In concluding his description of the LCS, Stricker writes succinctly that '*Every clinician engages in evidence-based practice. Indeed, it would be both foolish and professionally irresponsible to knowingly ignore any available evidence*' (2007, p 97). In common with other parts of this book, the conclusion here rests in the balance between two extremes; the clinical psychologist would be well-served to adopt research as a 'state of mind' (Cooper and Graham, 2009), and not be intimidated by a perceived need to regularly publish high-impact research articles.

In everyday practice, research skills can be useful in the provision of psychological therapy (think about how you learn to improve as you move through your career) but also in monitoring and evaluating performance through service evaluation and audit. Rather than being seen as an impediment to care provision, it could be argued that patients deserve transparency about services and indeed benefit from continued refinement of practices. If a service does not evolve, not only will it fail to improve, but it will also fail to respond to the changing demographics of its patients.

Modern training in Clinical Psychology supports this view. Over the course of my three years of professional training, for example, we trainees completed research projects including single-case experimental designs, service evaluations, literature reviews, and a large-scale research project that comprised our thesis. Since this time, I have used these skills within my clinical practice to audit service performance against published standards, evaluate the effectiveness of the treatments we provide, and (in an ambitious project) conduct a randomised controlled trial based entirely within an NHS service. I present these examples not to intimidate but rather to illustrate how accessible research can be, given the right mindset, motivation, and support.

6.4: PRACTICE SUMMARY

The importance of service evaluation

Service evaluations seek '*to assess how well a service is achieving its intended aims*' (Twycross and Shorten, 2014, p 65). They are an important means of evaluating performance and can help staff better understand their service and identify opportunities for improvement. They also promote transparency.

If you are working for a health service (or any organisation, for that matter), consider how you know whether what you are doing is effective or not. Is it evaluated? Do the metrics used reflect its actual performance? Are there any gaps?

As psychologists, we are well placed to design and conduct service evaluations and consider the impact of the findings more widely.

The research process (whether within a predominantly 'academic' or 'clinical' environment) can be time-consuming and, at times, confusing. One has to identify an appropriate 'gap' that needs addressing (primarily through a literature review), develop hypotheses, plan a project, obtain ethical approval, collect and analyse data, and then present the findings (see, for example, Cooper and Graham, 2009, pp 52–4). However, when given the right support (which, admittedly, may at times be lacking), it is amazing what can be achieved – and the importance of such work. I have benefitted from supportive bosses and supervisors, as well as discussions with people who 'have been there before'. We all had to start somewhere and my general impression is that most people are more than happy to offer advice when considering a research project; they won't do the work for you, but can save you a lot of time and effort by imparting lessons drawn from their considerable experience.

Despite the merits that clinical research can offer, it is also incumbent upon clinical psychologists to be heavily involved in this. As Thomas et al (2002, p 286) noted: '*If clinical psychology does not reassert its own research credentials, its evidence base in the future may be constructed more by psychiatrists, physicians and nurses than by clinical psychologists.*' Such contributions perhaps need to go beyond service evaluation and audit as, important though these activities are, they are usually specific to a local service and therefore have limited national and international impact, meaning that it is hard for practising clinical psychologists '*to develop strong research profiles*' (Thomas et al, 2002, p 287).

Having completed the doctorate, clinical psychologists are well-equipped to carry out research, this having been a core element of their training (BPS, 2019). Some clinical psychologists will move into full-time academic posts and have research at the forefront of their career. It is therefore sensible to consider what balance you might like in your career, and if a purely academic route might be indicated.

PHD OR DCLIN?

Some of those looking for a career in Clinical Psychology might consider doing a PhD. As mentioned in Chapter 1, the two (in the UK at least) are not the same: a PhD does not confer the clinical training inherent to the Doctorate in Clinical Psychology but rather provides research training, in some cases within an area relevant to Clinical Psychology. It does not (in the absence of a distinct qualification) allow one to practise as a clinical psychologist in the UK (ie, a PhD does not lead to status as a Chartered Clinical Psychologist). However, if you are strongly attracted to research within Clinical Psychology, then the PhD route may be for you (see Practice Summary 6.5).

PhDs are undertaken at universities and generally involve joining an established research group with the aim of conducting a research project to progress knowledge within a given field. Alongside a supervisor (typically a senior academic with an interest in Clinical Psychology), you will identify key objectives of your study and attend relevant training, such as courses on advanced statistics and research methods. PhD training therefore equips graduates to pursue influential positions within academia, industry, or as independent researchers.

Some people end up being 'double-doctors'. In many ways, this affords the best of both worlds – with both career options open to you. However, it is not for the faint-hearted and may also involve financial considerations. (Although PhDs are not paid in the same way as trainee clinical psychologists, they typically attract funding covering fees and a stipend.) Ultimately, your career may evolve in a certain direction which leads coherently to a doctoral degree. Alternatively, you may choose a different career, and we will cover some of these later, in Chapter 8.

6.5: PRACTICE SUMMARY

A PhD in Clinical Psychology: Alternative, adjunct, or altogether different?

As briefly noted earlier, some individuals applying for the Doctorate in Clinical Psychology have achieved a doctoral degree, namely a PhD. In the UK, this is a research degree not inherently leading to registration as a psychologist. Some individuals will choose to complete further training, such as that in Clinical Psychology, but the majority of PhD graduates will pursue careers in research – which may or may not be aligned to Clinical Psychology.

(continued)

A question often asked of me by students is 'which route should I choose?' Although both are possible, the training behind each is different and results in a different set of skills, albeit some of them overlapping. Many clinical psychologists have become prominent researchers and many PhD graduates have done hugely influential work with clinical samples, although it is generally the case that those with a professional doctorate will work as 'clinicians' whereas those with a PhD will become 'researchers'.

The obvious difference is that the Doctorate in Clinical Psychology is necessary for practice whereas a PhD isn't required to conduct high-quality research (although its comprehensive schooling in research skills is undoubtedly an asset). Both can lead to rewarding careers, although it is worth thinking about which is the best 'fit' for you.

SUMMARY

The discussion of tensions between research and clinical practice continues, and it is summarised here due to its impact on a number of everyday decisions facing the clinical psychologist. However, it may be wise to heed the words of Alan Kazdin, Sterling Professor Emeritus of Psychology and Emeritus Professor of Child Psychiatry at Yale University, who notes that '*No one is really well served by this debate and the split of research and practice. Perhaps the greatest casualty is the public at large*' (2008, p 147). While I would not dismiss concerns about use of evidence-based practice, resolution might come in the form of artistic application of science, which I have mentioned above. By keeping the interests of patients uppermost and using the best available knowledge, we can look to reduce the harms caused by interventions and maximise the potential to do good.

If all of these issues seem overwhelming, don't worry – you're not alone in feeling this way. The next chapter offers suggestions of how to maintain balance in one's life during a career which can feel all-consuming, and is an important consideration at any stage in one's professional life.

REFERENCES

APA (2006) Evidence-Based Practice in Psychology. *American Psychologist*, 61: 271–85. [online] Available at www.apa.org/pubs/journals/features/evidence-based-statement.pdf (accessed 6 July 2020).

Bennett-Levy, J, Butler, G, Fennell, M, Hackman, A, Mueller, M and Westbrook, D (eds) (2004) *Oxford Guide to Behavioural Experiments in Cognitive Therapy*. Oxford: Oxford University Press.

Blaine, C (nd) What Does Evidence-Based Actually Mean? [online] Available at: https://bestpractice.bmj.com/info/toolkit/discuss-ebm/what-does-evidence-based-actually-mean/ (accessed 6 July 2020).

BPS (2019) *Standards for the Accreditation of Doctoral Programmes in Clinical Psychology*. Leicester, UK: BPS. [online] Available at: www.bps.org.uk/sites/www.bps.org.uk/files/Accreditation/Clinical%20 Accreditation%20Handbook%202019.pdf (accessed 6 July 2020).

Cipriani, A, et al (2018) Comparative Efficacy and Acceptability of 21 Antidepressant Drugs for the Acute Treatment of Adults with Major Depressive Disorder: A Systematic Review and Network Meta-Analysis. *The Lancet*, 391: 1357–66.

Cohen, L H (1979) The Research Readership and Information Source Reliance of Clinical Psychologists. *Professional Psychology*, 10(6): 780–5.

Cooper, M and Graham, C (2009) Research and Evaluation. In Beinart, H, Kennedy, P, and Llewelyn, S. (eds), *Clinical Psychology in Practice* (pp 46–58). Chichester, UK: BPS Blackwell.

Court, A J, Cooke, A and Scrivener, A (2017) They're NICE and Neat, But Are They Useful? A Grounded Theory of Clinical Psychologists' Beliefs About and Use of NICE Guidelines. *Clinical Psychology and Psychotherapy*, 24: 899–910.

Dunning, D, Heath, C and Suls, J M (2004) Flawed Self-Assessment: Implications for Health, Education, and the Workplace. *Psychological Science in the Public Interest*, 5(3): 69–106.

Evidence-Based Medicine Working Group (1992) Evidence-Based Medicine: A New Approach to Teaching the Practice of Medicine. *JAMA*, 268: 2420–35. [online] Available at: www.cebma.org/wp-content/uploads/ EBM-A-New-Approach-to-Teaching-the-Practice-of-Medicine.pdf (accessed 6 July 2020).

Eyding, D, et al (2010) Reboxetine for Acute Treatment of Major Depression: Systematic Review and Meta-Analysis of Published and Unpublished Placebo and Selective Serotonin Reuptake Inhibitor Controlled Trials. *BMJ*, 341: c4737.

Frank, G (1984) The Boulder Model: History, Rationale, and Critique. *Professional Psychology: Research and Practice*, 15(3): 417–35.

Green, V A, Pituch, K A, Itchon, J, Choi, A, O'Reilly, M and Sigafoos, J (2006) Internet Survey of Treatments Used by Parents of Children with Autism. *Research in Developmental Disabilities*, 27, 70–84.

Insel, T R (2015) Transparency. [online] Available at: www.nimh.nih.gov/about/directors/thomas-insel/blog/ 2015/transparency.shtml?utm_source=youth.gov&utm_medium=Federal-Links&utm_campaign=Reports-and-Resources (accessed 6 July 2020).

Kazdin, A E (2008) Evidence-Based Treatment and Practice: New Opportunities to Bridge Clinical Research and Practice, Enhance the Knowledge Base, and Improve Patient Care. *American Psychologist*, 63(3): 146–59.

Kendall, P C (1998) Empirically Supported Psychological Therapies. *Journal of Consulting and Clinical Psychology*, 66(1): 3–6.

Lilienfeld, S O (2010) Can Psychology Become a Science? *Personality and Individual Differences*, 49: 281–8.

Lilienfeld, S O, Ritschel, L A, Lynn, S J, Brown, A P, Cautin, R L and Latzman, R D (2013a) The Research-Practice Gap: Bridging the Schism Between Eating Disorder Researchers and Practitioners. *International Journal of Eating Disorders*, 46, 386–94.

Lilienfeld, S O, Ritschel, L A, Lynn, S J, Cautin, R L and Latzman, R D (2013b) Why Many Clinical Psychologists Are Resistant to Evidence-Based Practice: Root Causes and Constructive Remedies. *Clinical Psychology Review*, 33: 883–900.

Lilienfeld, S O (2019) What is 'Evidence' in Psychotherapies? *World Psychiatry*, 18(3): 245–6.

Medicines and Healthcare Products Regulatory Agency (MHRA) (2011) Reboxetine: benefit-risk balance reviewed. [online] Available at: www.gov.uk/drug-safety-update/reboxetine-benefit-risk-balance-reviewed (accessed 6 July 2020).

Morrow-Bradley, C and Elliott, R (1986) Utilization of Psychotherapy Research by Practicing Psychotherapists. *American Psychologist*, 41(2): 188–97.

National Institute for Health and Care Excellence (NICE) (2020) What We Do. [online] Available at: www.nice.org.uk/about/what-we-do (accessed 6 July 2020).

Parry, G, Cape, J and Pilling, S (2003) Clinical Practice Guidelines in Clinical Psychology and Psychotherapy. *Clinical Psychology and Psychotherapy*, 10: 337–51.

Peterson, D R (2000) Scientist-Practitioner or Scientific Practitioner? *American Psychologist*, 55(2): 252–3.

Popper, K (1970) Normal Science and Its Dangers. In Lakatos, I and Musgrave, A (eds), *Criticism and the Growth of Knowledge* (pp 51–8). Cambridge, UK: Cambridge University Press.

Rosen, G M and Davison, G C (2003) Psychology Should List Empirically Supported Principles of Change (ESPs) and Not Credential Trademarked Therapies or Other Treatment Packages. *Behavior Modification*, 27(3): 300–12.

Sackett, D L, Rosenberg, W M C, Gray, J A M, Haynes, R B and Richardson, W S (1996) Evidence Based Medicine: What It Is and What It Isn't. *BMJ*, 312: 71–2.

Salkovskis, P M (2002) Empirically Grounded Clinical Interventions: Cognitive-Behavioural Therapy Progresses through a Multi-Dimensional Approach to Clinical Science. *Behavioural and Cognitive Psychotherapy*, 30: 3–9.

Shapiro, M B (1967) Clinical Psychology as an Applied Science. *British Journal of Psychiatry*, 113: 1039–42.

Southam-Gerow, M A, Weisz, J R and Kendall, P C (2003) Youth with Anxiety Disorders in Research and Service Clinics: Examining Client Differences and Similarities. *Journal of Clinical Child and Adolescent Psychology*, 32(3): 375–85.

Stricker, G (2007) The Local Clinical Scientist. In Hofmann, S G and Weinberger, J (eds), *The Art and Science of Psychotherapy* (pp 51–8). New York, NY: Routledge.

Thomas, G V, Turpin, G and Meyer, C (2002) Clinical Research Under Threat. *The Psychologist*, 15(6): 286–9.

Tobin, D L, Banker, J D, Weisberg, L and Bowers, W (2007) I Know What You Did Last Summer (and It Was Not CBT): A Factor Analytic Model of International Psychotherapeutic Practice in the Eating Disorders. *International Journal of Eating Disorders*, 40: 754–7.

Tversky, A and Kahneman, D (1974) Judgment Under Uncertainty: Heuristics and Biases. *Science*, 185(4157): 1124–31.

Twycross, A and Shorten, A (2014) Service Evaluation, Audit and Research: What is the Difference? *Evidence Based Nursing*, 17(3): 65–6. [online] Available at: https://ebn.bmj.com/content/17/3/65 (accessed 6 July 2020).

Walfish, S, McAlister, B, O'Donnell, P and Lambert, M J (2012) An Investigation of Self-Assessment Bias in Mental Health Providers. *Psychological Reports*, 110(2): 639–44.

Waller, G, Stringer, H and Meyer, C (2012) What Cognitive Behavioral Techniques Do Therapists Report Using When Delivering Cognitive Behavioral Therapy for the Eating Disorders? *Journal of Consulting and Clinical Psychology*, 80: 171–5.

7 Life beyond Clinical Psychology

If you have purchased this book (or had it bought for you, or borrowed it from a friend, or come to it intentionally through some other means), then it is perhaps a safe assumption that you are at least considering becoming a clinical psychologist. The preceding chapters have covered many diverse features of a career in applied psychology, and so this chapter devotes some time to the period following completion of professional training and the demands of being a qualified clinical psychologist. Many people pay insufficient thought to what actually happens after the award of a Doctorate in Clinical Psychology, but my view is that the training is only a beginning – a period of intense study preparing you for a journey that will hopefully extend long beyond graduation day. The working life of a clinical psychologist can be demanding, so this chapter will also cover the importance of having a good work–life balance, and how to manage some of the mandates that are given to you.

It is worth emphasising that qualifying as a clinical psychologist is not the end; it is the beginning. As we will see in the next chapter, there are a number of career opportunities available, whether working in the NHS, another part of the healthcare sector (such as private practice), social care, in education, or academic settings. However, as one's journey through the doctoral course emphasises, ongoing training and development (known widely in the UK and elsewhere as continuing professional development, or CPD) are integral to the working lives of practising clinical psychologists. In common with other professional bodies, the British Psychological Society (BPS) mandates that clinical psychologists produce a record of CPD activities to help them *maintain and enhance their professional skills whilst also maintaining public confidence in the profession'* (BPS, 2010). However, evidenced learning activities are only one part of further development.

THE GOOD WITH THE BAD

I love being a clinical psychologist. However, many aspects to the job are common to a number of similar professions and do not necessitate the specialist skills that epitomise Clinical Psychology. For example, working for any large organisation, such as the NHS, necessarily involves what is known as mandatory training. This is essential from both a legal and, more importantly, safety point of view and helps ensure that staff are sufficiently knowledgeable to maintain a healthy and safe working environment. However, many staff balk at the prospect of mandatory training, seeing themselves as sufficiently competent in an area (interpersonal communication or information governance, say) or simply struggling to find time to prioritise such training beyond other pressing commitments.

Whether you see mandatory training as worthwhile or not, you will be expected to do it and this can be seen as taking up time that could be spent in other areas ('*I could be treating patients now!*'). Similarly, other everyday tasks, such as responding to emails, attending meetings, and rearranging appointments also take up a lot of one's time. The point of raising this is to prompt you (if you are contemplating working in this area) to consider how you deal with all of the stresses you might face – not just those that might immediately come to mind, such as waiting lists or hearing traumatic life histories. Stress at work can have a huge impact, both in human and financial terms, and it is therefore crucial that, as psychologists, we not only attend to this but actively take steps to improve employee wellness – both our own and that of others. As Research Summary 7.1 below illustrates, clinical psychologists are exposed to many stressful aspects of the job early in our careers (it is one good reason to get practical experience prior to applying for training); this is also something we share with colleagues from other professions – within healthcare and beyond.

7.1: RESEARCH SUMMARY

A study of stress in trainee clinical psychologists

In a study authored by Jones and Thompson in 2017, face-to-face interviews were conducted with a total of 16 trainee clinical psychologists based at two different UK universities. The researchers asked questions about the participants' lives as clinical psychologists and paid attention to whether the trainees mentioned issues relating to stress. Although this was not probed for, three key themes of the trainee experience related to stress emerged, specifically:

1. The relationship between supervisor and trainee.
2. 'Imposter syndrome' – related to a fear of not being 'good enough'.
3. Support networks (eg, peers, work–life balance).

These themes were consistent across both samples and also reflected previous research in the area, suggesting that training in Clinical Psychology is demanding and also related to the coping abilities of each individual. Many trainees in this study described maintaining a healthy work–life balance, although the article points out that there may be some potential clinical psychologists who '*will be unable to marshal sufficient personal resilience to act as a buffer to the many stresses that such training brings*'. As with many studies in this area, it highlights potential stressors but also ways in which individuals cope with these.

Source: Jones and Thompson (2017)

The well-being of clinical psychologists

Thankfully, some recent work has begun to address the welfare of healthcare workers, in recognition of the fact that such careers are emotionally demanding and that the well-being of staff is closely related to patient outcomes and safety. To illustrate some of the potential impact, a survey conducted in 2012/13 found that 15.9 million days of NHS time were lost due to sickness (HSCIC, 2013), with mental health services consistently among the most severely affected. Furthermore, the NHS reports greater absence than many other sectors and, of even greater concern, healthcare professionals have some of the highest rates of suicide for any occupational group (Kelly et al, 1995). According to the 2018 NHS Staff Survey (a survey sent annually to NHS staff), 40 per cent have felt unwell as a result of work-related stress in the previous 12 months and more than half came into work in the previous three months despite not feeling well enough to perform their duties (detailed data are available online from www.nhsstaffsurveyresults.com/).

In order to investigate the issue of well-being in healthcare staff further, a collaboration between the New Savoy Partnership and BPS Division of Clinical Psychology resulted in a collection of annual surveys, completed by more than 1,000 healthcare staff in the UK. Key findings are summarised in Research Summary 7.2.

7.2: RESEARCH SUMMARY

Key findings in the Workforce Wellbeing Survey

o Levels of self-reported depression varied from 40 per cent (2014) to 48 per cent (2016).

o An increase in self-reported experience of stress with over 80 per cent of staff reporting that they find their jobs stressful either 'some of the time' or 'all the time'.

o 40–50 per cent had felt like a failure over the past week 'some of the time', 'often', or 'all of the time'.

o 13 per cent reported bullying and harassment from managers occurring once or twice in the past 12 months.

o Pay was unrelated to depression or stress at work.

Source: Rao (2019), Rao et al (2018)

Interviews with participants suggested that increasing negativity around working conditions was a result of services experiencing greater pressure, with respondents feeling unable to offer a reasonable standard of service. Further, they often saw their work as increasingly 'mechanical', with an emphasis on meeting 'targets', an aspect to work that has been particularly linked to poorer health outcomes (Goh et al, 2015).

This report is useful in drawing attention to the stresses that can occur because of one's job, and it highlights the significant levels of pressure existing within environments advocating the importance of health. Although many work-based demands are – to an extent – 'normal', persistent or excessive stress can result in an individual's threshold being breached and lead to greater absence and ill-health. In the following section, I have suggested a few domains to consider when reflecting on what your triggers might be, alongside consideration of your own character and what areas you might consider when trying to improve wellness.

WHEN STRESS BECOMES PERNICIOUS

One of the most widely applied theories of stress and coping is based around the cognitive appraisal model of Lazarus and Folkman (1984). In brief, the theory argues that individuals appraise stimuli in their environment, and that any subsequent reaction is dependent on how the particular stimulus is seen. If the stimulus is viewed as 'negative' (eg, threatening, potentially harmful), then individuals will respond with ways of coping which change the environmental conditions and trigger a reappraisal. If the threat has diminished (or the outcome is favourable), a positive emotion is experienced (Folkman, 1997) and no further action is needed. If the negative stimuli persist (or if others result), further coping skills may be enlisted and the appraisal cycle is repeated. There is room for individual differences within this and the theory offers an explanation why people respond differently to a similar, stressful event or why the same individual might respond differently to the same stressor at other times.

Continuing stress can lead to substantive changes in psychology and physiology (mind and body), and there appears to be an established relationship between work-related stress and negative health outcomes, such as cardiovascular disease (eg, Goh et al, 2015). However, workplaces have also offered the opportunity to investigate interventions to reduce the impact associated with stress, and there is huge financial benefit (in addition to the obvious human benefit) to investing in staff health and well-being (Rao et al, nd). Some of the most common recommendations include having a supportive management structure, supporting people to seek help when needed, and keeping staff informed. Although not all stress (at work or anywhere else) can be removed, effective management can lead to better outcomes for both employees and the employer; in the case of healthcare services, patients will benefit from this as well.

Working in healthcare can present a number of different stressors (see Practice Summary 7.3), although their impact will be mediated by individual characteristics (see, for example, Michie, 2002). I do not plan to synthesise the many research findings which have been generated over the years but will instead provide some reflections on what has

7.3: PRACTICE SUMMARY

Possible sources of work-based stress for NHS staff

- o Workload and being asked to do too much
- o Bullying and harassment
- o Discrimination
- o Lack of job security
- o Physical danger
- o Limited, or insufficient, resources
- o Emotional impact of the work
- o Feeling like one has little or no input into important decisions

Data from the NHS Staff Survey suggests that around a third of staff experienced unrealistic time pressures 'often' or 'always'; 7 per cent of staff experienced discrimination from patients or other members of the public and 8 per cent from colleagues. Over 25 per cent disagreed with the statement that they had '*adequate materials, supplies, or equipment*' to do their job and 56 per cent felt that their organisation acted '*fairly with regard to career progression/promotion*'.

helped me manage the challenges of working as a clinical psychologist, and will also put these in the context of some empirical findings.

SOCIAL SUPPORT

As I have touched on through the preceding chapters, support from other people has been vital in keeping me on track during my career. Friends and family can help you cope when life gets tough and it is impossible to become a fully rounded practitioner without the support of others. Although other people were instrumental in my education and early work as an assistant psychologist, I shall focus here on getting through the doctorate itself, not least as the lessons will apply more widely.

As noted above, my course had an 'intake' (class size) of 19 and three of these individuals and I became particularly close over the three years. Much of this closeness was developed through the shared experiences presented by clinical training, but we also shared other interests, such as going to music festivals, a love of travel, or just relaxing in front of the TV. There is also a more general sense on the course that you are all 'going through it together'. I have found such amity to be ubiquitous throughout the NHS, and this is often something that people will cite when asked how they deal with the pressures of work.

Outside of academic and clinical work, friends I met through sports were supportive and it was useful to have at least one interest that lay wholly outside of Clinical Psychology training. My main piece of advice to anyone pursuing this career would be to ensure that you have other areas (be it a hobby, sport, partner, family, social circle) that can take your focus away from your primary occupation.

7.4: EXERCISE

How do you cope?

Write down some strategies you currently use to help you cope. When you get stressed (with work or study, for example), what helps you manage? This might include strategies to relax (such as exercise or arts and crafts) or could be more about how you manage demands in general – for example, making lists or breaking down big tasks into smaller ones.

Some forms of coping can be more generic than others. Susan Folkman (eg, 1997) gives the example that 'meaning-focused' coping (such as drawing on religious beliefs or values) tends to be less situation-specific than something like coming up with a solution to a particular problem. Do you have coping strategies that can work in many situations, or some which work better at certain times than others? Do you have a few really useful strategies, or many?

Once you have done this, consider whether these strategies are robust enough to continue to use in your future career. Will they help you through a training course like the Doctorate in Clinical Psychology? Can you see them helping when you are working?

OCCUPATIONAL EXCESS

One reason why having distractions in my life has been so important is that I have, at times, been guilty of loving my job *too* much. Most of the time, this affords great pleasure, and there are certainly worse problems to have. However, positive as this can be at times, it is an issue that requires management. Incidentally, although reasons aren't given, nearly 60 per cent of NHS staff in the allied health professions reported working additional unpaid hours, and this is likely to be closely related to the high levels of stress reported.

In many careers, it can be difficult to draw a distinction between work and recreation; one example for me is writing research articles. Although it seems easy to file this in the 'work' tray, keep in mind that writing articles and publishing them (including editing, submitting to journals, responding to peer reviews) is rarely part of one's core job role in the NHS. (Even in academia, this is a task that often gets pushed to the margins of one's salaried time.) This is regrettable, but is often seen as an extraneous activity, albeit one that contributes to the profession more widely. I sometimes use writing to relax but am always clear why I am doing this and work to ensure that I have time for activities which I find purely recreational.

Similarly, commitment to clinical work can mean that it's easy to see 'just one more patient' but this can quickly become overwhelming and not only compromise the clinician's health, but that of the patient too. Thus, learning to say no is a core skill that I continually try to develop.

LEARNING TO SAY NO

As a big fan of efficiency, I have learned that taking on too much can become not only overwhelming but can also compromise productivity. Perhaps it is an example of self-justification, but I try to consider the implications of taking on another task in light of those that are already ongoing and how much effort I can devote to the new one. Doing more does not always equate to doing more well, and there are – as the cliché goes – only so many hours in the day.

At times, however, you may be asked to work 'out of hours' (a term generally referring to hours other than Monday to Friday 9–5, give or take). It is an uncomfortable truth, but it is rare that I have consistently worked to the 37.5 hours for which I was contracted (in line with the Staff Survey findings mentioned above). I don't resent this and, as the section above suggests, I am often happy to do it. However, I always thought it important to have boundaries around my working time, otherwise it would be quite possible to drive oneself into an early retirement or, more commonly, extended sick leave. I never adopted any particular 'rules' around this but had general principles which helped guide me in such situations. If there were critical issues that needed addressing, I would rarely hesitate to 'go the extra mile' and stay later than planned, but if things could be deferred until the next working day then doing so seemed like the preferred option.

In healthcare, it is rarely, if ever, possible to complete every task; there are always more patients to see, and more paperwork to do. If a patient presents at high risk (which can occur at any time), then one has a professional obligation to ensure a 'duty of care'. However, this needs to be balanced with one's own competencies regarding patient care. I was once told of a psychologist who was so concerned about a patient's safety that they arranged regular telephone calls over the weekend (when the clinician was not scheduled to be at work); there are doubtless situations where this is unavoidable, but in my experience these are exceedingly rare and often best handled by another professional (such as someone working in a Crisis Team). Many NHS staff with whom I have worked are deeply committed to helping patients; however, unclear boundaries around this can spill over into murky territory and can actually have detrimental consequences.

ROUTINE VERSUS FLEXIBILITY

The final point I wish to comment on here (although there are many more which could be covered) is the importance of establishing balance between having a fixed routine and being flexible with demands. Flexibility will help manage the hassles of work, enabling one to take breaks when the opportunity arises and to maximise efficiency. However, I have also found a degree of rigidity to be of use: I had certain times of the day which I would set aside for given tasks and used patient contacts to afford a degree of structure (conveniently, these appointments tend to occupy discrete one-hour chunks, which helps planning).

As the working world evolves, this dialectic becomes even more relevant. For example, more and more people are choosing to work flexibly, with employers encouraged to support requests for flexible working. There is some evidence, for example, that the ability to work from home is positively related to job satisfaction (PwC, 2016), allowing people to work at a time and place in which they feel most productive. Of course, working from home can be impractical (and may be open to abuse) but workers often cite greater flexibility and control over their environment as important factors in wanting to be more independent. Workers need to be trusted to do their work when not being 'watched' but this can also build trust in the employer, potentially resulting in happier – and more productive – workers. However, there is a dark side to this; those working flexibly might be expected to be available 24/7 and struggle with the separation between work and home lives.

Much of the literature in this area seems to converge on the theme of control, a variable that can be manipulated to one's advantage even on a small scale. For example, a 2014 article in the *Harvard Business Review* (Hoskins, 2014) remarks on a survey finding that '*workers whose companies allow them to help decide when, where, and how they work were more likely to be satisfied with their jobs, performed better, and viewed their company as more innovative than competitors that didn't offer such choices*'. Hoskins gives the example of tech companies who work with employees to design individual workspaces tailored to personal preference. Admittedly, work hammocks aren't going to be available through NHS Procurement just yet, but think about how you can control where you work – even in small ways.

A LIFE OUTSIDE CLINICAL PSYCHOLOGY

Throughout your career, it is important to keep a sense of perspective. You will likely experience professional setbacks and, while these are difficult to accept at times, having a variety of interests will help not only to deflect some of the disappointment but will also remind you that there are other things from which you can draw encouragement. Exercise 7.5 presents an exercise commonly used in CBT treatments for eating disorders which can afford some perspective.

Hopefully this chapter has been more encouraging than daunting. The idea of raising some of the challenges is to not only encourage you to see the full picture but also to consider – at an early stage where possible – what resources you have to cope when

7.5: EXERCISE

What is important to you?

In this exercise, you are invited to think about what is important to you and to think about your own self-worth.

First, take a few minutes to think about how you judge your own self-worth. If you are struggling, think about what is important to you. Examples might include relationships, work, a hobby, and so on.

When you have made a list of around six or seven different areas (this doesn't have to be the exact number!), rank them in order of importance. One way of doing this is to ask: 'If something goes wrong in this area, how much does it affect me?'

Next, draw an empty pie chart (a circle) and, starting with your first area, give each of the areas you have listed a 'slice' of the pie. Take a look at this. Does it look balanced? Are there activities you would like to spend more (or less) time doing? Do you need to redraw your pie chart to gain more balance?

Doing an exercise like this can help you reflect on what is important to you and consider whether there is a good balance. If work, for example, occupies a large slice, that might be fine – but it can be risky. If something goes 'wrong' in this area, are there other parts of your life that can keep you feeling positive?

Source: Adapted from Fairburn (2008)

times get tough. Of course, difficulties at work aren't unique to Clinical Psychology and so this chapter may be of use whatever path you choose to take. The next chapter will cover careers that have some similarities to Clinical Psychology and may be of interest.

REFERENCES

BPS (2010) *Continuing Professional Development Guidelines*. Leicester, UK: BPS.

Fairburn, C G (2008) *Cognitive Behaviour Therapy and Eating Disorders*. New York, NY: Guilford Press.

Folkman, S (1997) Positive Psychological States and Coping with Severe Stress. *Social Science and Medicine*, 45: 1207–21.

Goh, J, Pfeffer, J and Zenios, S A (2015) The Relationship between Workplace Stressors and Mortality and Health Costs in the United States. *Management Science*, 62: 608–28.

Hoskins, D (2014) Employees Perform Better When They Can Control Their Space. [online] Available at: https://hbr.org/2014/01/employees-perform-better-when-they-can-control-their-space (accessed 6 July 2020).

HSCIC (2013) Sickness Absence Rates in the NHS: January–March 2013 and Annual Summary 2009–10 to 2012–13. [online] Available at: https://digital.nhs.uk/data-and-information/publications/statistical/sickness-absence-rates-in-the-nhs/sickness-absence-rates-in-the-nhs-january-to-march-2013 (accessed 6 July 2020).

Jones, R S P and Thompson, D E (2017) Stress and Well-Being in Trainee Clinical Psychologists: A Qualitative Analysis. *Medical Research Archives*, 5: 1–19. [online] Available at: https://journals.ke-i.org/index.php/mra/article/view/1455 (accessed 6 July 2020).

Kelly, S, Charlton, J and Jenkins, R (1995) Suicide Deaths in England and Wales, 1982–92: The Contribution of Occupation and Geography. *Population Trends*, 80: 16–25.

Lazarus, R S and Folkman, S (1984) *Stress, Appraisal, and Coping.* New York: Springer.

Michie, S (2002) Causes and Management of Stress at Work. *Occupational and Environmental Medicine*, 59: 67–72.

PwC (2016) Work-Life 3.0: Understanding How We'll Work Next. [online] Available at: www.pwc.com/ee/et/publications/pub/pwc-consumer-intellgience-series-future-of-work-june-2016.pdf (accessed 6 July 2020).

Rao, A (2019) A New Deal for Staff: Are We Ready to Deliver on Sustainability and Transformation Plans? *Findings from the 5th Annual NSP/BPS Workforce Wellbeing Survey.* [online] Available at: www.bps.org.uk/sites/bps.org.uk/files/Member%20Networks/Faculties/Leadership/DCPLM_240419_Amra%20Rao%20Blog%20Wellbeing.pdf (accessed 6 July 2020).

Rao, A, Bhutani, G, Clarke, J, Dosanjh, N and Parhar, S (nd) The Case for a Charter for Psychological Wellbeing and Resilience in the NHS: A Discussion Paper from the Wellbeing Project Working Group Joint Initiative between the BPS and New Savoy Conference. [online] Available at: www.bps.org.uk/sites/www.bps.org.uk/files/Member%20Networks/Faculties/Leadership/The%20Case%20for%20a%20Charter%20-%20Discussion%20paper.pdf (accessed 6 July 2020).

Rao, A, Clarke, J, Bhutani, G, Dosanjh, N, Cohen-Tovee, E and Neal, A (2018) Workforce Wellbeing Survey 2014–2017. British Psychological Society, Division of Clinical Psychology & New Savoy Conference. [online] Available at: www.bps.org.uk/sites/www.bps.org.uk/files/Member%20Networks/Faculties/Leadership/2017%20Wellbeing%20Survey%20Results.pdf (accessed 6 July 2020).

8 Alternatives to Clinical Psychology

Clinical Psychology is certainly not the only profession for those wanting to work with psychological distress. To be sure, it is a great career, but the route in can be difficult and it is not for everyone. The current chapter discusses what alternatives exist outside of strictly defined Clinical Psychology and aims to give an overview of the main options that those interested in such work may wish to consider. Although there is not time to list all possible alternatives to Clinical Psychology (and, to those people wishing to know more, I apologise), I shall briefly discuss some other allied health professions (AHPs) before moving on to a more specific discussion of nursing, psychiatry, counselling psychology, and the relative newcomer of the psychological well-being practitioner (PWP).

ALLIED HEALTH PROFESSIONS

I feel I should state that it is certainly not my intention to 'gloss over' certain AHP roles, but it is difficult to comment fully on their core responsibilities and training given that my experience has only been indirect. The term AHP covers professions such as Art Therapy, Occupational Therapy, Podiatry, Radiography, and many more. Many practitioners work routinely in mental health, and all will likely have some contact with an individual suffering from psychological problems as part of their work. Personally, I have worked mostly with dietitians (for fairly self-evident reasons), physiotherapists, speech and language therapists, art therapists, and occupational therapists. I have also worked with social workers who have moved into healthcare as well as some more indirectly who work, for example, in local authorities or charities.

All of these careers share many commonalities, and individuals may have their own reasons for choosing such paths. It is often possible to train in a 'core' health profession and then move to another area of interest. It is quite common, for example, for individuals providing psychological therapy to have a background in nursing or as an allied health professional and to have completed further training (eg, postgraduate diplomas) in areas such as cognitive behaviour therapy (CBT).

Nurses make up one of the largest professional groups in the NHS, with over 300,000 working in the NHS across hospital, community, and primary care settings. Completion of an accredited nursing degree typically involves a mix of in vivo training and university study; in this way, it is similar to Clinical Psychology training. Nursing qualifications are based on specialism in one of four main areas (adults, children, learning disability, and mental health), but all courses comprise common foundation programmes, and we shall discuss this profession first.

MENTAL HEALTH NURSING

Mental health nurses often work in the community, outpatient or hospital settings, or residential units, helping provide treatment and care for people with a wide range of illnesses and complex presentations. One can see how such roles interact with those of the clinical psychologist, and nurses play an important role in delivering effective care; nurses develop rapport with patients (and their families), ultimately helping patients to take responsibility for their own care. They also occupy more specific roles, such as administering and reviewing medication, inputting into patient records and treatment plans, and organising activities (eg, social activities) to promote patients' health and well-being. In addition to working in traditional settings (such as one-to-one work on an inpatient unit), mental health nurses often take a lead on education and health promotion, and many use their experience to move into academia. In acute care, nursing skills are essential to the safe running of wards and guidelines exist on nursing requirements on mental health wards. Allied to this, nurses will often have a key role in following recommendations of the Mental Health Act (MHA), often staffing 'places of safety' where individuals detained under the MHA require admission.

In terms of qualifying as a mental health nurse, individuals must complete an approved course, such as a Bachelor of Nursing or Mental Health Nursing degree from a recognised university, although schemes for apprenticeship training are currently being rolled out. Mental health nurses are bound to uphold the professional standards of the Nursing and Midwifery Council (NMC), ensuring that patients receive high-quality care. Similar to guidelines for psychologists, mental health nurses are expected to apply their skills to a 'range of evidence-based individual and group psychological and psychosocial interventions… [and] carry out systematic needs assessments, develop case formulations and negotiate goals' (NMC, 2010). After qualifying as a nurse, there are opportunities to work in a variety of settings, remaining as a 'generalist' or choosing to move into a particular specialism.

As noted above, many qualified nurses working in mental health have obtained further qualifications and may work closely with clinical psychologists – often performing many of the same duties. Others go on to train as clinical psychologists, given the grounding in the areas covered above (eg, see Morrissey, 2015). In light of these similarities, differences include the respective approaches to the treatment of ill-health, requirements of professional bodies, and training backgrounds (eg, less direct exposure to psychological therapy).

PSYCHIATRY

When I was finishing secondary school and considering university courses, I thought about becoming a medical doctor. However, an A-level in Psychology sparked an interest that led me to conclude that, were I to study Medicine (and successfully complete the course) I would choose to pursue a career in Psychiatry and that maybe Clinical Psychology offered a more suitable alternative. As with Nursing, Medicine adopts a different philosophy to Clinical Psychology in terms of its treatment of distress. Allied with Nursing and, to an extent, Clinical Psychology, specialists in Psychiatry train in core areas of Medicine and then go on to practise in one of six sub-specialties (such as learning difficulties, forensic psychiatry, or child and adolescent psychiatry). They assist in the management of patients through a combination of measures such as medication, psychological treatments, social interventions, and physical treatment (eg, electroconvulsive therapy, surgical procedures). Specialist training in Psychiatry lasts for six years (after medical school and two years of foundation training), providing experience in the different areas of practice through training posts, typically lasting between four and six months. Within this, there is a minimum of 12 months spent in General Psychiatry. Many work towards a career as a Consultant Psychiatrist, where they are expected to provide support and leadership to teams, chair meetings, interview new staff, provide training and supervision, as well as preparing business plans and developing services (RCPsych, 2017).

As can be seen by simply totalling up the years in training (by and large, five years of medical school plus two years foundation training plus six years of core training), Consultant Psychiatrists accrue a significant breadth of experience both within and outside of mental health. They are also encouraged to evaluate services and to have a good understanding of evidence-based practice and critical appraisal of relevant literature; again, there is significant crossover here with Clinical Psychology.

Although many psychiatrists will complete further training in psychotherapy (eg, CBT), a principal difference is the focus on 'physical' treatments, such as medication (which are generally unavailable to clinical psychologists).

COUNSELLING

Counselling is widely practised in the NHS and is recommended as a treatment for mild-to-moderate depression (albeit with some restrictions; see NICE, 2009), with evidence of efficacy for generic psychological problems (Hill et al, 2008). Contrary to lay parlance, counselling is not just a general term for 'talking therapies' but is a treatment in its own right, distinct from other psychotherapies. Counselling for depression, for example, is often delivered as a manualised treatment, usually with a discrete number of individual sessions. It is derived from person-centred principles and targets emotional and intra-personal problems, which are hypothesised to maintain low mood. Counselling has often been provided in GP surgeries (eg, see Greasley and Small, 2005) and, more recently with the inception of the UK IAPT programme, can be accessed across primary care (eg, see Aldridge, 2019). Charities and private organisations also provide counselling, and counsellors work with specialist services, such as oncology and genetic disorders.

In terms of training, counsellors generally have a diploma or degree (eg, in person-centred counselling) leading to professional registration and may have additional postgraduate experience. Professional training takes three to five years but can be supplemented by prior relevant experience. According to the British Association for Counselling and Psychotherapy, training must include *knowledge-based learning* (eg, psychological theories and their application), *therapeutic competences* (eg, reflective practice, use of supervision), and *research awareness*. Many staff will have the word 'counsellor' (or variant thereof) in their role title, and some roles may require a professional qualification, such as being a registered nurse or occupational therapist.

As with other professions, there is significant crossover with the work of a clinical psychologist and it may risk offence to be overly simplistic when trying to describe areas of difference. Training in counselling also involves tuition and placement-based practical learning. In line with many healthcare professions, training as a counsellor covers academic theory but has a strong emphasis on personal qualities rather than prior academic knowledge per se. Training can incur a number of costs such as private supervision and personal therapy, in addition to taking an accredited course. In general, counsellors focus on prevention and early intervention with psychological problems as opposed to psychological interventions, which are typically provided by psychologists, psychotherapists, nurses, or psychiatrists. As with other professions, counsellors see a wide range of individual problems but can also build on their training to pursue more specialist areas.

COUNSELLING PSYCHOLOGY

There is substantial overlap in the conceptual foundations of all the 'applied psychologist' professions (clinical, counselling, health, educational, occupational, forensic, neuro-, sport and exercise), and therefore similar facets to their practice, such as assessment and treatment, engaging in research and service evaluation, and supervision. Different streams can therefore cover similar areas. For example, educational psychologists predominately work with learning and behavioural problems in educational settings but also 'cross over' to the management of autism, and may work very closely with clinical psychologists. Again, it is not possible to cover all permutations of applied psychology in great detail, but we shall focus on Counselling Psychology as this is commonly considered as an alternative to Clinical Psychology (itself becoming a division of the BPS in 1994; Parry, 2015) and represents perhaps the most overlapping of all the disciplines covered here.

Around 10 per cent of UK registered psychologists are trained within Counselling Psychology (Farndon, nd), a discipline which concerns the integration of psychological theory with practice and aims to reduce distress and promote well-being by focusing on an individual's subjective experience. It requires self-awareness and competence in relating to people within a therapeutic context and also incorporates core skills such as formulation. Training is similar to that of Clinical Psychology, with the requirement of completing a postgraduate doctoral degree and subsequent registration with national regulators. However, there also exists an 'independent' route to qualification where applicants (who do not wish to, or cannot, undertake the professional doctorate) develop their own plan for training and submit assignments linked to national competencies criteria (see, for example, Jones Nielsen and Nicholas, 2016). The resultant qualification enables registration with the HCPC and eligibility for chartered membership of the BPS.

Counselling psychologists work in all areas of mental health, and are also employed within the prison service, civil service, and local authorities, among others such as charities. Of note, postgraduate training is not directly funded by the NHS and incurs course fees similar to other professions, such as counselling.

Clinical psychologists tend to work with individuals suffering from more 'severe' mental health problems, although both professions will work with both ends of the spectrum. The difference in training and theory is often described by suggesting that counselling psychologists tend to have a greater focus on wellness rather than illness, reflecting training that is perhaps more humanist or integrative in nature. However, many of these distinctions are *'perhaps of more rhetorical than factual value, since these beliefs are shared by many clinical psychologists'* (Parry, 2015, p 191).

A NOTE ABOUT CLINICAL ASSOCIATE PSYCHOLOGISTS

Clinical associate psychologists (CAPs) represent a new grade of applied psychologist in England, the role having been proposed to the BPS Membership and Standards Board in 2016. Training is (currently) through a one-year Master's programme (in either Psychological Therapies in Primary Care or Applied Psychology for Children and Young People; BPS, 2020) and, similar to roles within the Improving Access to Psychological Therapies programme discussed below, is based on a number of competencies and training standards.

It is often claimed that the role is 'between' that of an assistant psychologist and a clinical psychologist – performing some functions of the latter but within a narrower scope. For example, CAPs will undertake assessment, formulation, and intervention with patients across a variety of settings and work under the supervision of a clinical psychologist. The role was designed to expand the psychological therapies workforce to meet the growing demand for mental health support. There are currently only a few areas in England offering training (initially delivered across Cornwall), although this is currently under review and may be disseminated more widely in time, including through a degree apprenticeship scheme.

IAPT AND PWPS

In 2007, a new development for the provision of psychological therapy in the UK was announced, known as the Improving Access to Psychological Therapies (IAPT) programme. Following pilot work in 2006, the initial drive was to increase provision of psychological therapy for depression and anxiety disorders. As such, IAPT delivers only evidence-based, nationally recommended treatments, particularly focused on CBT although others (eg, interpersonal psychotherapy, brief psychodynamic therapy) are also available. IAPT recruits two main types of practitioner: high-intensity therapists and psychological well-being practitioners (PWPs). PWPs focus on 'low intensity' interventions, such as guided self-help and behavioural activation. They also provide supervision to trainee PWPs and hold management roles. PWPs also work across specialisms and also have the opportunity to engage in post-qualification training. Their training is based on a national curriculum covering common mental health conditions and training courses are accredited by the BPS. Postgraduate courses typically last around one year and trainees are employed by the NHS, completing academic work and supervised practice. It is also possible to train through an integrated undergraduate degree – four years in duration with on-the-job training alongside clinically focused teaching.

High-intensity therapists, by contrast, deliver psychological therapy to people with moderate-to-severe depression and anxiety disorders. They usually have a background in a core profession (eg, nursing, social work) but others can access this career. For both high-intensity therapists and PWPs, there is similarity with the other vocations covered above; training is a mix of university study and clinical work, requiring a number of standards to be met. The IAPT programme has seen significant development in the first decade of its life, and it is possible (well, probable) that the service, and thus roles within it, will continue to evolve.

Given the remit to work with depression and anxiety (although some areas will treat other disorders), working in IAPT can be more specialist than other professions. The con here is that it is rare for a PWP to work intensively with a mixed caseload of the variety that might be seen by a clinical psychologist, for example. As with other professions, although teaching and research are encouraged, this is perhaps seen as more central to the identity of a clinical psychologist.

Table 8.1 summarises the key features/pros and cons of working within the disciplines discussed in this chapter. However, as mentioned above, it should be noted that this is only a summary and cannot cover all possible aspects of the roles. Similarly, many features (such as working in mental health, or directly with patients) are applicable – to a greater or lesser extent – to all, and the information provided is discussed in a relative manner. There are also many other roles available in healthcare (eg, occupational therapy, social work) which I have not covered, but may be of interest. The NHS Health Careers website (www.healthcareers.nhs.uk/) has some further information.

Table 8.1 Key features of different healthcare professions

Discipline	Pros	Cons
Clinical Psychology	Funded postgraduate courses Good job opportunities Work across the lifespan and different conditions/illnesses Work with individuals, couples, groups Strong ties to academia/research Good level of pay through career	Quite significant postgraduate training after 'first' Psychology degree High level of competition, particularly for postgraduate training Strong research and clinical skills expected

Table 8.1 (*Cont.*)

Discipline	Pros	Cons
Psychiatry	Potentially better working hours than other areas of medicine Often seen in higher levels of leadership and organisational management Higher pay relative to other care professions Specialties within psychiatry Use of both pharmacological and non-pharmacological approaches	Long training process Can involve significant shift and 'antisocial' hours working Significant responsibility (eg, status as Responsible Clinician, Mental Health Act Officer) Undergraduate medical degree essential
Nursing	Opportunity to work closely with patients Varied and flexible role – can pursue further training in a number of areas Good career opportunities/employment prospects	Can involve significant shift and 'antisocial' hours working Opportunities to provide psychological therapy may be more limited, particularly prior to further training Pay typically starts lower than other qualified roles (although training is typically shorter) Requires undergraduate degree
Counselling	Training usually shorter than other disciplines Focus on relationship with patients Variety of working environments (eg, GP surgeries, community centres, schools) Often see patients in the earlier stages of illness, before behaviours become more entrenched	Training is frequently unpaid and may necessitate obtaining therapy and supervision for yourself Extensive focus on personal development may be off-putting for some
Counselling Psychology	Variety of work and settings Focus on relationship with patients and use of psychotherapy to facilitate change Deep understanding of therapeutic processes and approaches	Requires self-financed postgraduate training or alternative qualification route Opportunities may be fewer than those within Clinical Psychology

(*continued*)

Table 8.1 (*Cont.*)

Discipline	Pros	Cons
IAPT/PWP	Relatively brief training timeframe (can be less than 12 months)	Focus on first-line evidence-based treatments, particularly CBT
	Work is very clinical in nature (ie, providing psychological treatments)	Early stages of career may be limited to a few conditions/illnesses
	Variety of working environments (eg, GP surgeries, community centres)	Can be a career 'ceiling', particularly for low-intensity practitioners
	Opportunities to specialise in other areas	

CHOOSING A CAREER

If you are reading this at the infancy of your career, you should take care to note that the discussion above certainly does not cover all possible routes. The focus is mainly on those within healthcare and similar in nature to Clinical Psychology (after all, it's unlikely that you are reading this book in the hopes of getting some insight into the world of hedge funds). In the end, the decision about where your career ends up will be with you. All the careers above offer flexibility and have relative costs and benefits compared to other roles, so it is worth thinking carefully about which might be best for you and if some practical experience could help provide insight.

Although my fall into Clinical Psychology perhaps owed more to serendipity than preparation, it is well worth investing time in thinking about where your interests, strengths, weaknesses, and passions lie. I now feel that Clinical Psychology works in tandem with my own personal strengths – I can manage academic demands, cope well under pressure, enjoy the symbiosis between scientific knowledge and clinical practice, appreciate diversity in my career, and benefit from being challenged. Importantly, I quite genuinely feel that a psychological approach is the best way to work with people and mental illness. While I am respectful of a more 'medical' model, I don't think that I could apply it with the same faith and passion with which I do psychological interventions. Although we often discuss evidence-based practice, psychological treatment is often about faith. It feels like a discomforting and 'dirty' analogy to make but, like marketing a useful product, one can perhaps better help people find what they need if one truly believes in the integrity and utility of what one is 'selling'. With this, I am not suggesting that psychologists, or other mental health professionals, 'peddle' talking therapies, but that it helps immeasurably to work in a field where you are passionate about helping people and encouraging them to find their own solutions within a framework that you yourself believe in.

8.1: EXERCISE

Which is right for me?

Have a think about the careers we have just reviewed and perhaps include a couple more. Write down what you know about each and whether this is a route you might consider. There might be some you dismiss immediately but are there others about which you would like to know more? Think of some ways you could find out more – like going on a website of a relevant professional body or looking at training courses and their content. Are there any services near you where these professionals work and could you make contact with them to learn more?

If you're struggling to develop a clear career focus (and I hope this book goes some way to helping), give it some thought. You may want to look at what job possibilities exist, although accurately forecasting this will be tricky. Have a think about what really interests you and where your personal strengths and weaknesses lie. What do other people say about you? What attributes would those closest to you (honestly) list? Perhaps some of the best advice is to go out and find work experience, whether this is on a voluntary basis, part-time, or in another country. As well as acting as a demonstration of your commitment if you stay in that area, this will also help you learn what you like, and what you don't. Think you like working with children? Try to find some teaching assistant experience in a school. Tempted by academia? Ask at the local university if there are any projects with which you could assist. If you think you like charity work, consider approaching a non-governmental organisation or another part of the non-profit sector. Some Psychology degrees offer work placements or 'sandwich' years, and these can be really helpful in shaping your career. Sometimes, learning what you don't like is as important as learning what you do.

WORKING TOGETHER

In over ten years working as a psychologist, I have truly appreciated input from a range of colleagues. While I cannot profess to always having agreed with them, diversity of thought is an essential ingredient in driving change and improving quality. My strengths within a team have often been complemented by those of others – where I am weak in an area, they show a strength that moves the team along. When I was managing a team within the NHS, we had a great dynamic – it was founded on mutual respect but allowed each individual to showcase their own strengths while contributing to the larger goal. This is a precious, and at times delicate, balance but – to my mind – homogeneity is the enemy of progress; as such, different professionals and viewpoints will naturally bring about challenge to the orthodoxy, and drive improvement.

As can be seen above, there are many commonalities across healthcare roles (and we haven't touched on the huge contribution of those in 'supportive' roles such as administrative staff, nursing and healthcare assistants, and so on). However, each has its own contribution and Clinical Psychology offers a balance between being person-centred and scientifically based, within an overarching approach which works well for me. My support for Clinical Psychology should not be seen as criticism of other professions – all can make a difference for both individuals and wider society – but I *am* attempting to describe how the unique approach of Clinical Psychology fits well with my views of people in need, and how to help them. It is not the case that 'one size fits all', and so I recognise that the approach I favour has limitations; this is a key reason why multidisciplinary working is so integral to a functioning team. Although not the preserve of the clinical psychologist, seeing people every day who have endured truly horrible pasts and wish to change their own world for the better makes for sobering reflection; that I can assist with this is a great privilege.

AN INDIVIDUAL STANCE

If you have benefitted from psychological therapy in the past, you may have felt that the tools used during treatment worked particularly well for you because they 'made sense'. Another therapeutic approach may have helped you equally well, but these same tools don't always work for everyone and there is some evidence for 'equivalence' of different treatment options across patients (although this is a very contentious and complex area of healthcare research).

Just as there are different professionals within healthcare, so there are different ways of practising within any one profession. In their respective approaches to psychological therapy, clinical psychologists cite a diverse range of therapeutic orientations (see Norcross and Karpiak, 2012). Although there is clearly room for changing one's mind, there is some evidence that preference for one therapy is associated with decreased preference for another (eg, Buckman and Barker, 2010).

However, it is not just in psychotherapy that passion and enthusiasm for one approach should resonate with the clinical psychologist. As we've seen, at the heart of practice in Clinical Psychology lies the scientist-practitioner approach (see Chapter 6), which can add further diversity to one's career as there are many ways to embody this approach. Clinical psychologists, in common with many of the other professionals mentioned in this chapter, can find themselves pursuing a more academic route, a largely clinical route, or a mixture of both. A number of studies support the finding that the modal number of published articles for clinical psychologists is zero, although the majority have published at least once and the median number is around eight (Norcross and Karpiak, 2012). These findings stand in stark contrast to the recommendation for clinical psychologists to be sufficiently skilled in conducting research, an issue that was covered in Chapter 6, but also shows that there are many ways to be successful in one's career; some have argued that it would be a 'mistake to equate clinical psychology research productivity with output of trained psychologists' (Thomas et al, 2002, p 287).

If you choose to pursue a career in Clinical Psychology, it may be that the profession I am describing today is not the same which you enter. However, I believe that the fundamental skills in which clinical psychologists are trained serve them well to cope with new environments, and the next chapter considers what changes the discipline might face in time.

REFERENCES

Aldridge, S (2019) Counsellors in IAPT. [online] Available at: www.england.nhs.uk/blog/counsellors-in-iapt/ (accessed 6 July 2020).

BPS (2020) Clinical Associates in Applied Psychology. [online] Available at: www.bps.org.uk/public/become-psychologist/related-roles-and-careers (accessed 6 July 2020).

Buckman, J R and Barker, C (2010) Therapeutic Orientation Preferences in Trainee Clinical Psychologists: Personality or Training? *Psychotherapy Research*, 20: 247–58.

Farndon, H (nd) HCPC Registered Psychologists in the UK. [online] Available at: www.bps.org.uk/sites/www.bps.org.uk/files/Policy/Policy%20-%20Files/HCPC%20Registered%20Psychologists%20in%20the%20UK.pdf (accessed 6 July 2020).

Greasley, P and Small, N (2005) Evaluating a Primary Care Counselling Service: Outcomes and Issues. *Primary Health Care Research & Development*, 6(2): 125–36.

Hill, A, Brettle, A, Jenkins, P and Hulme, C (2008) *Counselling in Primary Care: A Systematic Review of the Evidence*. Lutterworth: British Association for Counselling & Psychotherapy. [online] Available at: www.bacp.co.uk/media/1973/bacp-counselling-in-primary-care-systematic-review.pdf (accessed 6 July 2020).

Jones Nielsen, J D and Nicholas, H (2016) Counselling Psychology in the United Kingdom. *Counselling Psychology Quarterly*, 29(2): 206–15.

Morrissey, S (2015) My Journey from Nurse to Psychologist. *InPsych*, 37(6). [online] Available at: https://psychology.org.au/inpsych/2015/dec/feature/morrissey (accessed 6 July 2020).

National Institute for Health and Care Excellence (NICE) (2009) Depression in Adults: Recognition and Management. [online] Available at: www.nice.org.uk/guidance/cg90 (accessed 6 July 2020).

NMC (2010) *Standards for Competence for Registered Nurses*. London: NMC. [online] Available at: www.nmc.org.uk/globalassets/sitedocuments/standards/nmc-standards-for-competence-for-registered-nurses.pdf (accessed 6 July 2020).

Norcross, J C and Karpiak, C P (2012) Clinical Psychologists in the 2010s: 50 Years of the APA Division of Clinical Psychology. *Clinical Psychology: Science and Practice*, 19: 1–12.

Parry, G (2015) Psychologists as Therapists: An Overview. In Hall, J, Pilgrim, D and Turpin, G (eds), *Clinical Psychology in Britain: Historical Perspectives* (pp 181–93). Leicester: BPS.

RCPsych (2017) PSS Information Guide: From Trainee to Consultant. [online] Available at: www.rcpsych.ac.uk/docs/default-source/members/supporting-you/pss/pss-guide-8.pdf?sfvrsn=585ad3ac_2 (accessed 6 July 2020).

Thomas, G V, Turpin, G and Meyer, C (2002) Clinical Research Under Threat. *The Psychologist*, 15(6): 286–9.

9 Looking forwards

Predicting the future, especially that of a profession as diverse as Clinical Psychology, is always a risky business. This chapter casts a circumspect eye on where the field may find itself in five or ten years, considering this in the context of national (and international) training and the constantly evolving field of healthcare. There are many pressures on the field – financial, demographic, political, and so on – and thinking about these may help ensure that the profession of Clinical Psychology is well-placed to continue to evolve.

WILL THERE STILL BE CLINICAL PSYCHOLOGISTS?

Emphatically, yes! Hopefully, this book has helped you see the value of clinical psychologists within healthcare and the contribution that they make across many areas of society. The profession is valued within the British Psychological Society (BPS) and also by other influential organisations, including falling firmly within long-term plans for the NHS. Recent plans from the UK Government have put mental health as a priority and professional groups, such as the BPS Division of Clinical Psychology and Association of Clinical Psychologists, have made arguments for the continued expansion of Clinical Psychology services. The need for clinical psychologists and the skills they offer will remain for some time.

However, the profession itself is likely to see some changes in the coming years. For example, as mentioned in Chapter 8, the NHS in England is currently training clinical associate psychologists (CAPs), a new grade of applied psychologist. The role is similar to – although distinct from – the clinical applied associate psychologists (CAAPs) run in Scotland since 2005. Concerns have been raised about this role – for example that it might 'devalue' Clinical Psychology, add confusion to patients and other healthcare professionals, and stifle professional development. However, CAPs may prove to be an important asset in the delivery of healthcare to the general population, improving the provision of psychological care in particular.

Advancement of other professional groups (eg, CAPs, PWPs) will surely lead to change in the role of the clinical psychologist and there does seem to be a trend (highlighted by other authors, such as Llewelyn and Aafjes-van Doorn, 2017) of psychological therapy to be increasingly provided by those without doctoral qualifications. The type of work done is likely to remain the same but the proportions of this (see, for example, Chapter 1) might shift. Given that the contribution of clinical psychologists goes over and above psychological therapy, this should not pose a problem, but it does require those of us who wish to see this profession thrive to consider what we offer and evolve within the changing landscape. Many of the possible drivers for evolution of the profession are, perhaps predictably, financial in nature, so it is worth covering some of the ways that Clinical Psychology is affected by the financial climate of society at large.

THE CHANGING FINANCIAL LANDSCAPE

At the time of writing, and for many years prior, the main 'consumer' of Clinical Psychology services was the NHS, an organisation which almost immediately following its conception faced crucial discussions about its financial viability.

The economic arguments that plague the NHS are too complex to delve into here but an understanding of the healthcare context is of relevance. The main area of spending of the NHS is staffing and so there is a pressure for individuals and their professions to justify their contribution. This may seem heartless but, commanding such a large slice of the NHS fiscal pie, even small changes to staff costs can have a significant systemic impact. Clinical psychologists are currently paid at Band 7 and, as noted earlier, this reflects the skills needed and requirements of the role. In comparison to other professions, this is relatively well-paid and there are also opportunities for growth. Clinical psychologists must therefore continue to demonstrate their usefulness and emphasise their role in services going forwards.

There is a felt pressure among some colleagues that their role within the NHS is becoming more complex and varied than it used to be. While this is welcome news in terms of the potential for change it can bring, it is also associated with additional stress, role blurring, and staff burnout. In 2014, the British Association for Behavioural and Cognitive Psychotherapies released a statement describing concern that their members (including psychologists) were expected '*to meet unrealistic service contracts*' (www.babcp.com/About/Press/Bullying-Culture-in-NHS-Mental-Health-Services-Putting-Vulnerable-Patients-at-Risk.aspx) and, as noted earlier, excess demands are often reported in staff surveys and are strongly related to stress.

How the future of NHS finances will evolve is anyone's guess. Suffice it to say that most, if not all, professions will come under scrutiny at some point and will need to show their value to the health service if they are to thrive. While this can often seem like an intangible threat, or one that lies at someone else's feet, I believe that it is the responsibility of every clinical psychologist to safeguard the integrity and strength of the profession; this is a big ask, of course, but it is necessary for Clinical Psychology to have another 100 years of influence.

THE STATUS OF CLINICAL PSYCHOLOGY

It has been remarked before (eg, Baker et al, 2009) that practitioners of Clinical Psychology are at risk of being their own worst enemy. Baker et al (2009, p 67) argue that clinical psychologists currently operate in a '*prescientific*' manner, '*valuing personal experience over scientific research'*. As we saw in Chapter 6, others have put forth the view that there are two 'worlds' within Clinical Psychology – one that prizes scientific evidence, and another that consists of *'mental health professionals who routinely neglect research evidence'* (Lilienfeld et al, 2015, p 1).

The irony here, noted earlier, is that the discipline of Clinical Psychology was founded on the 'scientist-practitioner' model, promulgating academic rigour and the weight of evidence. The evolution of formulation-based approaches has sometimes been suggested as a reason to deviate from evidence-based treatments, but the two need not be incompatible. Indeed, it is perhaps more likely that clinical psychologists are uncomfortable with some (perceived) aspects of evidence-based treatment, not the general principles. What is of concern is that the unique contribution of Clinical Psychology to healthcare might be lost if we allow ourselves to discard that which is most characteristic of this profession.

The 'three-legged stool' is an analogy that has been used to summarise a key approach to evidence-based practice. Reflecting the themes covered in this book, the idea is that clinicians are encouraged to make decisions considering: (1) the best available research evidence; (2) clinical expertise; and (3) patient characteristics, perspectives, and opinions (eg, Peterson et al, 2016). Its approach is perhaps best summarised in one of the most influential articles in the field:

> *Without clinical expertise, practice risks becoming tyrannised by evidence, for even excellent external evidence may be inapplicable to or inappropriate for an individual patient. Without current best evidence, practice risks becoming rapidly out of date, to the detriment of patients.*
>
> (Sackett et al, 1996, p 71)

Clinical Psychology is well-placed to implement this model, given the training focus on evaluation of available scientific evidence, clinical expertise, and the importance of the patient in the therapeutic relationship. However, practitioners differ in the relative weighting they afford to each 'leg' and some surveys suggest that research findings play only a minor role in therapists' clinical decision-making (eg, Gyani et al, 2014).

I will not repeat the arguments around this issue here (see, for example, Lilienfeld et al, 2013) but suffice it to say that the uncomfortable truth is that clinical intuition, while not to be ignored, often falls short of actuarial prediction in terms of accuracy and judgement. Further, many practitioners are overconfident in their abilities and ignore the same psychological processes about which they are tasked with educating others (eg, see Lilienfeld et al, 2014). There is a risk, then, that the role of clinical expertise is given paramount support, perhaps to the neglect of the other two 'legs'. Communication between those involved in an individual's care is essential and can reduce the possible conflict that can result when patient and professional hold divergent views about diagnosis and treatment (see, for example, Siminoff, 2013).

British psychologists such as John Hall, John Marzillier, Tony Lavender and others have written along similar lines. Following an initial formulation of an individual (see Chapter 2),

9.1: EXERCISE

How do you see the future?

Take a moment and think about the healthcare system where you live – both locally and nationally. Have you seen any changes recently – perhaps to funding or a shift of emphasis towards, or away from, certain health conditions? Have you noticed anything reported in the media about this? Now, consider that you might be working for a local service – what are the challenges now, and how might these be different in a few years' time? Where might you be able to help and how do you see this role?

Clearly this exercise is hypothetical but it can be useful to visualise yourself in a specific role and think about how, and where, you would like to make a difference.

Hall and Marzillier (2009) suggest that one of five options are open to the practising psychologist: (1) No treatment; (2) Creating a therapeutic alliance; (3) Seeking social and community support; (4) Providing a specific psychological intervention; and (5) Help by another profession. All too often psychologists are expected to 'default' to Option 4, on the assumption that a patient's experience can be distilled to a diagnostic label and an appropriate treatment thus provided. However, there is a nuance to this choice, where a different outcome can still result in cost-effective treatment, but with the additional benefit of really involving the patient and helping them come to a decision that places them at the centre of their care.

CHALLENGING THE STATUS QUO

One truism about human beings is that they will often hold their beliefs even when faced with strong evidence to the contrary; indeed, some beliefs even become more firmly held when challenged (see, for example, now-classic experiments such as Anderson et al, 1980). And so it is with evidence-based practice in Clinical Psychology (Lilienfeld et al, 2013). Much like changing someone's mind about important social attitudes (such as the role of capital punishment; see Lord et al, 1984), 'persuading' a clinician to adopt an evidence-based approach may be futile and can often only be accomplished through subversion, threats, or other nefarious means. However, reflecting the evidence base for psychological treatments itself, Clinical Psychology is dynamic; the current 'leading treatment' for, say, panic disorder might not be the promoted treatment in 20 years' time. The evidence base necessarily changes over time, possibly in line with social norms, and clinical psychologists are well-placed to respond to this, given their consideration of societal context, social pressures, physical health, and so on.

As a result, clinical psychologists should be questioning about evidence and use the scientific approach to reflect on their own biases and evaluate their own practice (eg, see Lilienfeld et al, 2017, and Chapter 6). Too many whom I meet feel afraid of challenging what they read and are taught and shy away from an empirical approach. Despite training in literature reviewing and statistical methods, many clinical psychologists feel ill-equipped to refute a line of evidence on a given treatment. A study's findings are only as strong as the method behind them, and sometimes these can be found wanting (for example, recall the discussion in Chapter 6 regarding reboxetine). The sheer volume of evidence now available at the click of a mouse can feel overwhelming but leads to the conclusion that psychologists need to use their skills more than ever to evaluate the full picture of evidence, including a review of the original studies' methodologies. Writing in 1998, Davison (p 166) reflected that, as psychologists, '*we learned to critique articles published even in the most prestigious of journals, to view pronouncements of what is true or valid with a jaundiced eye, to question authority, and to be continually on the look-out for conceptual, methodological, and statistical flaws in everything we read, say, and write*'. I see these words not only as reflective of the ideals to which (clinical) psychologists should aspire but as a guide to what we can offer to the implementation of evidence-based practice.

The controversy around evidence-based practice in Clinical Psychology will likely continue for many years to come, but compelling views towards a solution have been advocated by several authors. A combination of approaches is likely to be needed (see, for example, Lilienfeld et al, 2013) although a helpful analogy is provided by Schön (1983), describing similarities between mental health professionals and architects (admittedly, two quite disparate professional groups). Schön describes how architects are trained in the fundamentals of, say, building design and learn their trade by studying several exemplars. They build on this (no pun intended!) to develop their own style but must always remember the basic principles of architecture. As Schön notes, both architect and mental health professional approach problems as individual cases but do not '*act as though [they] had no relevant prior experience*' but, rather, seek '*to discover the particular features of his problematic situation, and from their gradual discovery, designs an intervention*' (p 129).

In Clinical Psychology, there is, in places, a schism developing between those adherent to implementing the evidence base and those more sceptical of the relationship between research evidence and clinical practice. This poses a grave danger to the profession and may well engender a split, with individuals at varying stages of their careers forced to choose sides. However, while evidence-based treatments offer '*unprecedented opportunity for facilitating the integration of science and practice in psychological therapy training*' (Calhoun et al, 1998, p 151), there remain those who object to the wholesale application of group-based findings (such as those obtained in RCTs) to individual cases, and thus shun the evidence base. A balance can be struck, however, by taking account of the evidence base (and its associated probabilities) and addressing some of the misconceptions about what evidence-based practice is and what it is not (see, for example, Lilienfeld et al, 2013). Collaboration between 'researchers' and 'practitioners' is one way of achieving this – exemplified in the approach of the clinical psychologist.

TECHNOLOGY AND CLINICAL PSYCHOLOGY

Another way in which clinical psychologists might find themselves needing to adapt is the changing world of *how* healthcare is delivered (as opposed to *what* healthcare is delivered, discussed above). There is the possibility that evolving technology (and other changes) will lead to less 'office-based' work and more working from home, and this is feasible for many aspects of the clinical psychologist's work. For example, many therapeutic interventions have now been moved 'online', adopting digital technology in the very delivery of psychological interventions.

Now a common element of modern Clinical Psychology textbooks (eg, Pomerantz, 2017), technology occupies a prominent position in many debates around healthcare. Clinical psychologists have a range of ways they might incorporate technology with their practice, such as videoconferencing in lieu of face-to-face sessions, providing psychological support via email, and supervising the use of online psychotherapy programmes. The promise of these advancements is tantalising – how many more people could access appropriate treatments if there was no need to attend a clinic in person? Similarly, the cost of delivering interventions is also diminished when they can be delivered via an online platform. However, the answer to the question of whether technology-aided psychological therapy 'works' is complex (Marks and Cavanagh, 2009) and this emerging field has also thrown up a number of important ethical issues.

Budding clinical psychologists will likely be educated and trained in an environment that is increasingly dependent on technology. Although not all clients will be as tech-savvy, the perceived practicality and economic advantages conferred by technology will likely be promoted as incentives to large healthcare organisations. Therefore, it is (or, certainly, will be) incumbent upon clinical psychologists to respond to this change and be prepared to adapt their practice when necessary.

As I highlighted at the outset of this book, those interested in pursuing a career in Clinical Psychology must be (perhaps above all else) adaptable. In few other areas is this likely to be as critical as when considering the delivery of healthcare alongside technology. It would be a shame if individuals were put off this profession for fear of technology 'taking over' but it is perhaps a reality that to evolve alongside the profession, one must embrace the changing face of healthcare delivery.

TRAINING IN CLINICAL PSYCHOLOGY

Although the philosophy and pedagogy of Clinical Psychology seems relatively invariant and is likely to experience only minor shifts, clinical psychologists may find themselves working more widely, such as in the domains of primary care and public health, as opposed to more 'traditional' settings involving mainly psychological therapy. Training may change to reflect this, although flexibility will still be required on the part of the clinical psychologist.

The future structure of training in the UK is subject to some debate. It may be that the current funding model is discontinued, with alternatives such as bursaries or other shared funding arrangements being considered. However, these may discourage the diversity that is so necessary to this profession, emphasise the marginalisation of certain groups, and even stifle innovation (eg, see Kinouani et al, 2015). Furthermore, there have been arguments that the current funding structure is appropriate given the postgraduate status, role of trainee clinical psychologists on placement, and the longer-term retention of clinical psychologists (eg, Lavender and Chatfield, 2016).

In response to concerns of threats to the funding of Clinical Psychology training, BPS Chief Executive Sarb Bajwa highlighted the complexity of funding of trainee clinical psychologists, surmising that it is '*vital that we don't make any changes to the current system that could negatively affect the future flow of psychologists into the NHS*' (www.hsj.co.uk/workforce/specialties-under-threat-from-potential-training-cuts/7024955.article). While the support of professional bodies is crucial, a solid base for supporting the thorough training of clinical psychologists is necessary to ensure that the quality, integrity, and character of the profession endures. There may well be alternative methods of training clinical psychologists, but it is critical for these to remain faithful to the founding principles and unique identity of the profession.

REPRESENTATION OF CLINICAL PSYCHOLOGY

At present, clinical psychologists are registered with the HCPC and many – but not all – are members of the British Psychological Society. The BPS can confer the title of Chartered Psychologist (CPsychol) to reflect individuals showing the highest standard of psychological knowledge and expertise. The BPS subdivision the Division of Clinical Psychology (DCP) is the traditional representative body of clinical psychologists although many responsibilities now lie with the HCPC (principally the statutory regulation of applied psychologists). As such, the DCP's mission is to '*support the development of Clinical Psychology, both as a profession and as a body of knowledge*' (www.bps.org.uk/member-microsites/division-clinical-psychology) and also hosts faculties such as intellectual disabilities and psychology of older people.

In 2017, the Association of Clinical Psychologists-UK (ACP-UK) was established as a professional body independent of existing structures with a vision of being '*a strong voice for clinical psychologists in the UK*'. The ACP, for its part, has explicitly called to work together with the BPS although the BPS retains a remit of promoting psychology as a discipline above any one particular group. It is yet to be seen how these two organisations will work together and how this will affect the make-up of Clinical Psychology in the UK but it is something to keep an eye on moving forwards.

CONCLUSIONS

Change is inevitable. The challenge for clinical psychologists is to embrace this while staying true to the unique foundations of our training. In my view, this shouldn't be too difficult – but one should not be complacent. In an era of financial austerity and a seemingly growing need for healthcare, the role of the clinical psychologist should be foremost, but it could also be passed over for alternatives – deemed by some to provide an equivalent service with fewer costs.

Through this book, we have covered what a clinical psychologist does (although this varies greatly), and how they are trained. We have also covered some challenges to the profession and what makes it unique. I hope that it has given you some ideas for reflection and perhaps answered some questions you might have had. Above all, I hope it invites you to learn more about the profession and, if you wish to pursue a career as a clinical psychologist, that it has provided some insight into what you might do next.

REFERENCES

Anderson, C A, Lepper, M R and Ross, L (1980) Perseverance of Social Theories: The Role of Explanation in the Persistence of Discredited Information. *Journal of Personality and Social Psychology*, 39: 1037–49.

Baker, T B, McFall, R M and Shoham, V (2009) Current Status and Future Prospects of Clinical Psychology: Toward a Scientifically Principled Approach to Mental and Behavioral Health Care. *Psychological Science in the Public Interest*, 9: 67–103. [online] Available at: www.psychologicalscience.org/journals/pspi/pspi_9-2.pdf (accessed 6 July 2020).

Calhoun, K S, Moras, K, Pilkonis, P A and Rehm, L P (1998) Empirically Supported Treatments: Implications for Training. *Journal of Consulting and Clinical Psychology*, 66(1): 151–62.

Davison, G C (1998) Being Bolder with the Boulder Model: The Challenge of Education and Training in Empirically Supported Treatments. *Journal of Consulting and Clinical Psychology*, 66(1): 163–7.

Gyani, A, Shafran, R, Myles, P and Rose, S (2014) The Gap Between Science and Practice: How Therapists Make Their Clinical Decisions. *Behavior Therapy*, 45: 199–211.

Hall, J and Marzillier, J (2009) Alternative Ways of Working. *The Psychologist*, 22(5): 406–8.

Kinouani, G, Tserpeli, E, Stamatopoulou, V and Nicholas, J (2015) Innovation: Another Case for Widening Access to Clinical Psychology? *Clinical Psychology Forum*, 266: 2–4.

Lavender, T and Chatfield, S (2016) Training and Staff Retention: National Issues and Findings from the Canterbury Christ Church University (Salomons Centre for Applied Psychology) Clinical Psychology Training Programme. *Clinical Psychology Forum*, 286: 31–8.

Lilienfeld, S O, Ritschel, L A, Lynn, S J, Cautin, R L and Latzman, R D (2013) Why Many Clinical Psychologists Are Resistant to Evidence-Based Practice: Root Causes and Constructive Remedies. *Clinical Psychology Review*, 33: 883–900.

Lilienfeld, S O, Ritschel, L A, Lynn, S J, Cautin, R L and Latzman, R D (2014) Why Ineffective Psychotherapies Appear to Work: A Taxonomy of Causes of Spurious Therapeutic Effectiveness. *Perspectives on Psychological Science*, 9: 355–87.

Lilienfeld, S O, Lynn, S J and Lohr, J M (2015) Science and Pseudoscience in Clinical Psychology: Initial Thoughts, Reflections, and Considerations. In Lilienfeld, S O, Lynn, S J and Lohr, J M, *Science and Pseudoscience in Clinical Psychology* (2nd ed, pp 1–18). New York: Guilford Press.

Lilienfeld, S O, Lynn, S J, O'Donohue, W T and Latzman, R D (2017) Epistemic Humility: An Overarching Educational Philosophy for Clinical Psychology. *The Clinical Psychologist*, 70(2): 6–14.

Llewelyn, S and Aafjes-van Doorn, K (2017) *Clinical Psychology: A Very Short Introduction*. Oxford: Oxford University Press.

Lord, C G, Lepper, M R and Preston, E (1984) Considering the Opposite: A Corrective Strategy for Social Judgment. *Journal of Personality and Social Psychology*, 47: 1231–43. [online] Available at: http://citeseerx. ist.psu.edu/viewdoc/download?doi=10.1.1.595.8173&rep=rep1&type=pdf (accessed 6 July 2020).

Marks, I and Cavanagh, K (2009) Computer-Aided Psychological Treatments: Evolving Issues. *Annual Review of Clinical Psychology*, 5: 121–41.

Peterson, C B, Black Becker, C, Treasure, J, Shafran, R and Bryant-Waugh, R (2016) The Three-Legged Stool of Evidence-Based Practice in Eating Disorder Treatment: Research, Clinical, and Patient Perspectives. *BMC Medicine*, 14: 69.

Pomerantz, A M (2017) *Clinical Psychology: Science, Practice, and Culture* (4th ed). Thousand Oaks, CA: Sage.

Sackett, D L, Rosenberg, W M C, Gray, J A M, Haynes, R B and Richardson, W S (1996) Evidence Based Medicine: What It Is and What It Isn't. *BMJ*, 312: 71–2.

Schön, D A (1983) *The Reflective Practitioner: How Professionals Think In Action*. New York: Basic Books.

Siminoff, L A (2013) Incorporating Patient and Family Preferences into Evidence-Based Medicine. *BMC Medical Informatics and Decision Making*, 13: S6.

10 Concluding notes

This wouldn't be a book on Clinical Psychology without some reflective comments at the end, but I shall try to keep them brief and, while admittedly self-focused, of relevance to individuals other than myself.

Modern Clinical Psychology is a wondrous thing. In my view, it offers solutions to many current problems within healthcare and beyond and provides an alternative to the predominant, often medicalised, view of mental health. However, it also risks losing its identity and, with it, its most important contributions.

Writing this book has been quite illuminating for me. It has helped me get back in touch with Clinical Psychology as a profession – something from which one can feel at times oddly estranged. This is perhaps due to my own unique situation but might also reflect how difficult it is to define Clinical Psychology due to its breadth, growth, and overlap with other fields. Similarly, the further one gets from training, the more one's career evolves and can diverge from the core principles of Clinical Psychology and the reflective scientist-practitioner approach. Learning more about the history of the discipline (thanks, largely, to the text of Hall et al, 2015) has helped put my opinions in some context and also provided some justification. For example, I have at times struggled to come up with a 'definition' of Clinical Psychology, a challenge that has not been overlooked in textbooks in this area (eg, Hall et al, 2015; Pomerantz, 2008).

Nonetheless, this book can also be seen as written from an 'internalist' position (eg, Hall et al, 2015, p 366); providing a summary of my own journey has limited the breadth of its coverage. I have tried to emphasise that the information presented is coloured by my own experiences and is therefore open to refutation. Similarly, what is known now may later be disproved. The information presented in this book (and that omitted) may also reflect a personal (and wider political) bias of how the world of healthcare and Clinical Psychology is seen. Inclusion of case studies and generous contributions from other individuals is an attempt to broaden the scope but adopting a Western perspective and, more acutely, that of a White, British male, has undoubtedly presented an Anglocentric view of the profession. Therefore, as with many areas of the book, readers are invited to challenge what is presented and look more widely for inspiration – whether this is through additional reading or more experiential endeavours.

This book has attempted to describe what life is like as a practising clinical psychologist, and I hope it has done that. It has also summarised the process leading up to professional registration and alternative career options. Even though its writing has felt at times like a marathon, there is a lot of information that I have not been able to include in the book, and some areas that I would have liked to have covered in more detail. These omissions are my responsibility and reflect – either intentionally or unintentionally – my choice of content. I hope that I have provided at least some avenues where more information can be found, although there are some areas where we simply need to know more. This is perhaps my challenge to aspiring clinical psychologists – try to break new ground. Look into areas of experience or knowledge where none has gone before you. Use the breadth of Psychology to create new ways of seeing things. Help those who are marginalised.

Other books in this area exist and I hope that many more are written in time. Clinical Psychology is a misunderstood vocation, but it is also one not given to self-promotion. I hope that this modesty is not its undoing and that those new to the profession will drive it forwards. To do so will take integrity, persistence, creativity, and flexibility – precisely the credentials valued within Clinical Psychology.

REFERENCES

Hall, J, Pilgrim, D and Turpin, G (2015) *Clinical Psychology in Britain: Historical Perspectives*. Leicester: BPS.

Pomerantz, A M (2008) *Clinical Psychology: Science, Practice, and Culture*. Thousand Oaks, CA: Sage Publications.

INDEX